Dayle E. Spencer

A gift for

_____

From

_____

Praise for Loving Spirit Self-help for the Journey of Loss

"Loss in our lives can often paralyze us, leaving us in need of a helping hand. With care and wisdom born of her own loss, Dayle E. Spencer offers a helping hand that encourages with empathy but is also clear that we can help ourselves. She shows us how."

-Bishop Minerva G. Carcaño
The United Methodist Church
Los Angeles

"*Loving Spirit, Self-help for the Journey of Loss*, is educational and inspirational. It is a practical guide that helps each of us on the journey of restoration, of healing, of life!"

-Rabbi Mark Blazer
Spiritual Leader, Temple Beth Ami
Founder, Albert Einstein Academies

"Dayle Spencer, an accomplished expert of change and crisis management, faced her own crisis with the loss of her beloved daughter. This she described in her remarkable memoir *Loving Allie, Transforming the Journey of Loss*. She sets out now to 'objectively reflect on some tools and techniques that were helpful in our journey and to share our healing process with others.'

That is an understatement. Ms. Spencer describes core elements of loss and how loss impacts all of us in complex and enduring ways. She observes through multicultural, intellectual and spiritual lenses. She lists in exercises and suggestions multiple ways of approaching ourselves.

Ms. Spencer is gutsy. She is passionate and unafraid to approach grief and loss from different perspectives--social, psychological, religious, spiritual and mystical. She describes her own very personal experiences and hones the tasks of the journey into practical exercises. I am struck throughout with her ability to help us see the universality of our experiences. She teaches us that we have encountered loss and change at every level of our development, we have learned from that and have become the better for it.

What is remarkable in this practical and straightforward book is the confidence and optimism in the reader. That he or she will encounter her grief, engage her loss and ultimately change to a new and healthy place."

-Gene Borkan, M.D., Psychiatrist

"A very readable, practical, and thought-provoking guide to navigate the many facets and dimensions of the grieving process, from someone who has personally (physically, emotionally and spiritually) lived through the experience of loss and sadness and emerged with a sense of peace and hope!"

- Very Rev. Gregory T. Bittner, J.D.
Catholic Priest, Pastor, Lawyer, Medical Ethicist

"As a trauma therapist, I have been honored to assist the healing journey of many people who have been blind sighted by some type of loss or drastic change in their lives. At such painful times, I view it as if life is a puzzle and many of the pieces have suddenly been tossed into the air to land in disconnected, new places. As Dayle Spencer explains, the brain has been wired from childhood to deal with our lives and now, nothing quite seems to have the same meaning or purpose. Your brain is in a state of anxious and/or depressed emergency trying to cope with the sudden distressing changes. Most people feel terribly alone and not understood even by those closest to them. Dayle Spencer tragically knows this state only too well after the sudden death of her daughter. She has respectfully and graciously shared her insights regarding how to understand and cope with such loss and created this workbook to guide you on your recovery to find your new normal."

-Robin Grant-Hall, Ph.D.
Trauma Psychologist

"*Loving Spirit, Self-help for the Journey of Loss,* is the most thorough and complete resource I've read (and experienced) in transitioning through the process/journey of transforming grief. It embraces our unique and diverse spiritual and cultural traditions that rise from the core of our common human experience and all-encompassing Loving Spirit. What a precious gift from the author's heart that becomes a living reminder and healing guide for all of us in this voyage of recovery and transformation through life. Mahalo nui loa! I will certainly recommend it highly to all my family, friends and colleagues."

-Rev. Piula Ala'ilima
Pastor, Wesley United Methodist Church, Honolulu

"After experiencing such an unimaginable loss, Dayle Spencer movingly shares her personal story. She offers insights about journeys we take after similar life-changing events. This tough self-help workbook is a vehicle for mourning and adaptation while honoring the lost loved one."

-Vamik D. Volkan, M.D.
Psychoanalyst
Author, *Life After Grief, The Lessons of Grief*

"*Loving Spirit* is a beautifully written guide to rediscovering joy in the crevices of loss. Rooted in Dayle Spencer's personal journey of grief and healing following the death of her daughter, Allie, it offers practical information, coupled with reflections and exercises, which guide readers towards a deeper understanding of themselves as they forge their own path to recovery and transformation. The work is challenging but the rewards arc invaluable."

-Devon Dabbs
Executive Director and Co-founder
Children's Hospice and Palliative Care Coalition

loving Spirit

Self-Help for the Journey of Loss

Dayle E. Spencer

BALBOA
PRESS

A DIVISION OF HAY HOUSE

Balboa Press books may be ordered through booksellers or by contacting:

Balboa Press
A Division of Hay House
1663 Liberty Drive
Bloomington, IN 47403
www.balboapress.com
1 (877) 407-4847

Print information available on the last page.

ISBN: 978-1-5043-2777-0 (sc)
ISBN: 978-1-5043-2779-4 (hc)
ISBN: 978-1-5043-2778-7 (e)

Library of Congress Control Number: 2015902390

Balboa Press rev. date: 4/1/2015

"The world breaks everyone, and afterward, many are strong at the broken places."
Ernest Hemingway

This book is dedicated to Allie,
whose loving spirit guided the writing of it.

Acknowledgments

I AM INDEBTED TO former President Jimmy Carter and former First Lady Rosalynn Carter, Dr. Beth Karassik, comedian and best selling author Louie Anderson, Barbara Findeisen, Dr. Anthony Elite, Dr. William Ury, and Dr. Norman Estin for their early support of my writing about recovery from grief.

Special thanks to the support team I've had at Balboa Press, including Alan Bower, Heather Carter, Stephanie McClure Cornthwaite, Brian Fox, Sarah Goddard, Brandon Kline, Nicolas Martel, Shelby Owen, Mary Wegener, and David Yoder.

Kathy Strickman provided invaluable editing support and guidance.

Sue Doylan provided early printing and moral support.

I am deeply indebted to Allie's good friends Doug Carney, Patty Tredway, Luisa Engel, Liz Ambrosia, Melissa Keeport, Anthony Pristyak, Melanie Grossman, Sarah Stewart, Vanessa Marsh, Rebecca Smith, Kareem Khubchandani, Susanne Brooks, Erica Keiter, Lucas Woodford, Danielle Allaire, Andrew Middleton, Gabe Russell, Polly Morton, and Sarah Yost, for their enthusiasm for this work, and for loving Allie.

Our friends Roy and Dorothy Christopher, Jessie and Dan Dugan, Louise and Mike McDonald, Ludie Dickeson, Susan and John Camphouse, and Betty Sakamoto read my early drafts and gave me their guidance. Donna and Frank Shavlik, Angela Vento, Julie Sherlock, Debbie Sperry, David Camphouse, Piula Ala'ilima, Andy Kilpatrick, Brandt and Josie Ayers, Howard Rifkin, and Sunya Schlea provided emotional support.

Thanks to Brent Schlea for his beautiful photography and to Lauren Gay for her efforts on my behalf.

My wonderful Star Sisters -- who have always been my soul support group - - Lea Flocchini, Christa Huseby and Nancy Miner gave me love and encouragement.

My beloved sons Geoff and Matt were always on my side.

And Will, as always, was my rock, my soul mate, my sounding board, a keeper.

Special thanks to Winston, who got up with me at 3:00am when I couldn't sleep because I was thinking about this book, and who patiently waited for the occasional breaks to toss a ball or go for a walk.

Contents

Introduction 1

A Word of Advice..4

What is the Journey? 11

Who Am I? 21

What is Grief?...30

What Has Been My Journey? 38

What is My Type? 45

How Does My Type Grieve?...52

What Do I Believe? 63

Loss Doesn't Render Us Powerless............................... 68

What Am I Mad About, Sad About, Scared About?.....79

Whom Do I Need to Forgive?......................................89

What Are My Resources? 96

Some Success Stories.. 111

One More Thing.. 119

Suggested Reading.. 121

About the Author 123

Introduction

*"What the caterpillar calls the end, the rest of the world calls
a butterfly."*   Lao Tzu

O
N JANUARY 2, 2011, my beloved daughter, Allison Lanier
Powell, died suddenly and unexpectedly from the flu.

It was not an unusual strain of the flu, just the common flu. Her
death came within thirty-six hours of being admitted to a hospital
in Boston after she fainted. We were thousands of miles away in a
remote beach house and couldn't get to her bedside before she died.

Allie's death was a seismic event in my life, shaking me to the very
core of my existence. I wrote about what that experience was like and
how I survived it in an earlier book called, *Loving Allie, Transforming
the Journey of Loss*. My hope was that by sharing a candid and frank
look at how this loss affected me that I might help others who were
grieving.

Some of the most important lessons I learned from Allie's death
resulted from two decisions my husband Will and I made almost
immediately. One was a choice not to view ourselves as victims, and
the second was a choice not to see her death as tragic. These choices
taught us that even when devastating loss comes our way we are
not powerless in its face. We have the option to decide how we will

respond to it, how we will think about it, and what amount of power we want to give it in our lives.

Because we had spent decades of our lives helping societies and individuals learn to manage conflicts and change, we knew that certain choices and mindsets would have great influence on our ability to recover from this overwhelming loss.

Societies sometimes assign an important value to a particular loss and use it to justify behaviors for years, or even generations thereafter. This is a kind of eye-for-an-eye rationale. The decision to make a trauma a primary focal point of one's life played out in the Deep South post Civil War, and nationally after the attacks of 9/11/2001, and continues to play out currently in the Middle East. People can choose to define themselves in ways that lock them into a relationship with loss. This notion that the loss becomes who they are is not a healthy self-image. It can become a rationale for many negative behaviors that are self-perpetuating. We found ourselves, after twenty years of consulting, having to take our own advice; choosing not to play the role of victims, and choosing not to "catastrophise" the loss. It was a painful and necessary pill to swallow.

Now, four years later, with the passage of time, and with the perspective that comes from hindsight, it is possible to objectively reflect on some tools and techniques that were helpful in our journey and to share our healing process with others.

This book is intended to be an easily accessible, affordable, and practical guide for those who have met a major loss of some sort. It is called *Loving Spirit* for many reasons. We need to love our essential spirit, our self. We are surrounded by the spirits of those who have gone before and who hold us in loving, supportive ways. We can be a force for good in the world, a loving spirit to those who are on the journey with us. And, we are all connected, spiritually, to the One loving spirit. This book seeks to come from a place of *Loving Spirit* as it addresses an assortment of self-help tools that can assist someone who has experienced a major loss.

Each Chapter begins with a saying by Lao Tzu, an ancient Chinese philosopher, who reputedly wrote the *Tao Te Ching* more than twenty-five hundred years ago. Whether he was an actual person, or the sayings are a compilation of wisdom by many authors, each attributed quote has stood the test of time. The *Tao Te Ching* had only 5,000 Chinese characters when it was written in 500 B.C. Yet it has been translated more than any other book except the Bible and it is still in print.

The exercises in this book may be hard for you to do. They may cause you to cry, or get angry, or want to walk away from the whole process. Believe me when I say I totally understand. It may be that the best way to do the work is in baby steps. Depending on where you are on your journey you may not yet be ready to tackle some of the exercises. Take your time. Go at your own pace. The point is not to have you simply complete the exercises like checking off items on a to-do list. Rather, the most benefit will come if you pace yourself, think deeply about what the issue is and give a considered response. You may need to stop periodically and just breathe for a while to slow down enough to absorb the meaning of the exercise. There is no one right way here, but hopefully doing the work will help give you some peace and new perspective.

While the book was begun as a response to a loss caused by death, it can be applied to almost any loss that renders us broken at our heart space, including divorce, change or end of career, health crisis, personal setback; in short, anything that causes a shift or redefinition of either the meaning, identity or structure of our lives.

Loss can be experienced as a catastrophic event, especially when it occurs suddenly or violently. My hope in writing this self-help manual is to make your loss more manageable and easier to bear. Please know that you don't have to go at it alone, nor should you. There are many good support groups, and community resources, including therapists, doctors, religious leaders, and friends and family who can give good counsel and advice. I used every one of these types of resources, including the suggestions contained herein as part of my own recovery journey.

For now, though, let's see how much help you can give yourself.

A Word of Advice

HIS IS MEANT to be a workbook. That means you have to work at it. If you do the work that is described herein it can help you navigate the journey of loss with greater insight, compassion, forgiveness, and ultimately a better outcome.

But some readers will rush the process. They will not even read the book; rather they will glance through it, glean a few points, and then put it away. My husband Will reads this way. Sometimes he even reads a book from the back to the front. He engages books with his headspace, not his heart space. If you are one of those readers, you will be shortchanging yourself in this process. This book is for healing your broken heart. The real benefit of the workbook is if you slow down enough with each exercise to allow yourself to both think and feel the importance of your answers.

I totally understand the rush, especially if you have just suffered a major loss and you are grieving. It is challenging to focus the mind under states of high stress. Grief is perhaps the greatest stressor so it is no wonder someone might have problems focusing on instructions or reading a self-help manual.

4

Buddha described our frantic states as having a monkey mind. A monkey mind is a mind that is overtaken by a bunch of drunken, screeching, clamoring monkeys running around stirring up anxiety and fear. He suggested that we meditate daily just to calm our monkey mind and to realize that our anxieties are mostly self-created. If you approach your grief process or the exercises in this workbook with a monkey mind you may overwhelm your psyche and actually end up worse instead of better.

Think of it like making a pot of French-pressed coffee. First you boil a kettle of water. Then you place the coarsely ground coffee in the bottom of that pretty glass coffee pot. Then you add the hot water and cover it with the presser lid. Then you wait. You must wait four minutes. If you don't wait, the coffee will be too watery and spoiled. However, if you can manage to do something to occupy your mind and your anxious hands for just a few minutes, then when you press the filter down into the bottom of the pot, voilà! You have made a perfect pot of coffee.

If you aren't one of those people who can slow down enough for a perfect pot of coffee, or use yoga, exercise, meditation, music, or other techniques to quiet your mind, let me suggest a method that worked for me when Allie died. It is coloring. Remember in elementary school when you were given a few crayons and a page and told to draw a picture? Well, coloring can still offer you a chance to express yourself and a means to manage your super-charged emotions. It is a non-fattening, no cholesterol, and non-addictive way to focus the mind and calm the spirit.

But you are an adult now, not a first grader. So I'm offering you four mandalas as an adult option for stilling yourself. A mandala is an ancient symbol of wholeness, a sacred circle. The word is from the Sanskrit, but mandalas have been found in many cultures throughout time, including, Hindu, Buddhist, Christian, Native American and Celtic, among others.

Just grab a few colored pencils and find a quiet place and color. If you will do this before you begin the workbook you may find that you have greater patience for the whole process. Then, later, if you put the book down for a while, when you come back to it you might reengage by coloring a second or third mandala before you begin a new section of the workbook.

This technique worked so well for me that I bought several books of mandalas for future enjoyment. They are my treasures. At the end of each coloring session at least you have made something beautiful. In times of grief, that alone can be an achievement.

It is a bit like talking a walk in nature and looking at the leaves, not just the trees. When you only see the forest, you are seeing the big picture, but are missing more of the story. Loss and grief are intimate, detailed, fragile, introspective and raw experiences. Our memories of what was lost often come down to small things, smells, smiles, gestures, and styles. We have to see the leaves. We have to slow down and go there to get through loss.

So please try the mandalas. If they don't work for you, try any other technique for slowing yourself down that does. Don't rush through the book, and don't make the mistake of thinking that you can rush through the journey of loss. It will take as long as it takes.

©Tisha Ardis/Shutterstock.com

©Tisha Ardis/Shutterstock.com

©Tisha Ardis/Shutterstock.com

©Tisha Ardis/Shutterstock.com

What is the Journey?

"The journey of a thousand miles begins with a single step."
Lao Tzu, *Tao Te Ching*

W E ALL DIE. And in most cases, we don't have any say in how, or when it will happen. The global population is now in excess of 7 billion people. According to the www.worldometers.info website which is based on U.N. data, more than 100,000 people died today. And of those 7 billion plus living right now, all of us will be dead in about 100 years.

In spite of the fact that our death is inescapable, most of us spend a lot of energy denying that it will happen to us. One of my friends and a former colleague, Dr. Vamik Volkan, calls ours a culture of death deniers.

Instead of saying that our grandmother or grandfather died, we use euphemisms to conceal the true nature of what happened. We say things like: "Grandmother went to live with God," or worse, "Grandfather is sleeping with the angels now," or "My brother passed yesterday," or "We lost our mother."

If this is how death is explained, is it any wonder that small children become afraid of the dark, or learn to fear God, or that adults feel they're to blame when someone they loves dies?

And if we don't even confront our own mortality, we certainly run from dealing with the frightening fact that everyone we know, and our entire family will die, too. Death does not discriminate. It takes us all.

Who among us can't recount a story of unnecessary suffering or heartbreak that was created by someone who was in denial of this simple reality? Many years ago, when one of my family members was terminally ill with lung cancer, I asked her to record a series of messages to her young daughter that might be shared with the little girl as she grew into womanhood. I offered to tape record them, or take down dictation, or do anything that would preserve some part of her mother's memory for the child. She died not long thereafter and her daughter grew up with almost no memory of her mother.

When Allie died, many people used the expression that I had lost my daughter and they were sorry for my loss. I bristled every time this was said because it seemed to imply negligence on my part somehow. Did I not watch her carefully enough? Had she wandered away, never to be seen or heard from again? No, she died. She simply died. She wasn't lost. She just died.

Her death was the start of my journey. Thus far, it has been a four-year journey from utter brokenness and almost unbearable pain to a place of greater acceptance, of developing scar tissue over the open wounds, of forgiveness, reconciliation and a return to a new normalcy.

Which begs the question when she died, what was lost?

I think the answer to this question is the same whether our loss is caused by a death or by some other major upheaval in our lives such as a divorce, or retirement, or career change or setback. To me, what I lost, at least for a while, was the meaning, identity and structure of my life.

The devastation of grief caused me to fundamentally question what my life had meant up to that point; was it being wasted, did I make the best use of my time and talents, would anyone care if I died, what had I stood for or stood against that mattered? If someone were writing about my life after I died, what would be the headline? And finally I came around to asking myself, what would be missed if my life ended tomorrow?

The identity part of my loss was trickier. I had identified myself as a mother of three children for almost thirty years by the time Allie died. When asked, I would quickly recount that I had two sons and a daughter. Since her death, I stumble when asked a question by any stranger about my children. Well meaning hair dressers, merely trying to make conversation, will say something as innocent as "*how many children do you have?*" And my mind does a kind of internal debate. Do I care enough about this person to tell her the whole story? Do I just say how many children I *have*, which is how the question was posed, or do I say how many children I *had*, which may be more than they wanted to know?

I was very clear that I didn't want my identity to become indelibly linked to death. Yes, I had a daughter who died. But more important to me than how or when she died was how she lived. Allie lived her life full out, exhausting herself with things to do and places to go and people to meet and love. She stuffed so much into twenty-eight years it was remarkable. She made friendships that lasted from early childhood until her death. She invested in relationships, slowing down and listening and caring about others. Instead of having my identity become that of a mother whose daughter died, I preferred to think of myself as a mother whose daughter really knew how to live, and who lived well her entire life. That would be something to celebrate, not mourn.

For three years after Allie died the structure of my life was almost complete chaos. We left our home in Colorado, merely locking the front door, giving away our dog, and getting on a plane for Maui. But once we arrived we never quite settled into the new structure of Maui life. We moved several times on Maui as we tried to regain our footing. And then we finally moved back to Colorado.

With so much of our lives in upheaval it was hard to find our center. Were we running from death or just running?

Relationships are Multi-dimensional

Part of the reason I felt so completely bereft was that I failed to understand what was actually lost and what remained from my relationship to my daughter after her death. My immediate conclusion was that I had lost everything; all of her, and it left me feeling pretty hopeless. With time, I came to see that our relationship was more complex than I originally thought and that while I had lost the physical aspect of it, I would no longer see her, or hear her voice, or smell her vanilla essence, I still had both an emotional and spiritual connection to her that death could not destroy.

Let me say that again in case you raced through it. When someone we love dies, we only lose the physical aspects of the relationship. Our emotional and spiritual relationship with them cannot be destroyed by mere death.

By working hard to understand and learn from the grief experience I came to see that when we are in a personal relationship with someone else, whether it's romantic, or familial, or close friendship, it's not just a physical relationship. Of course the physical aspect is important, as that is often the beginning of our feelings for the individual. We may find them physically beautiful or handsome. We may love looking into their eyes. We may enjoy their touch. We may find their sense of humor, or intelligence compelling. These are all physical aspects of our relationship. But relationships have other dimensions as well.

We have an emotional connection to those we love. These emotional ties begin even before birth in the case of expectant parents. Without ever seeing their child for the nine months of gestation, the parents can become completely emotionally attached as they await its birth. Parents who miscarry or whose child is stillborn will grieve as deeply as any others even though they may never had actually held their child or had much of a physical relationship to it. I feel strong emotional ties to friends I have known since law school. It causes me to care about their wellbeing, and even though we may not see each other often geographical distances do not weaken the emotional connection.

And we also have a spiritual connection to our loved ones. Depending on your spiritual belief system you may believe that you and your loved one were together before you entered this world. Some believe that spirits pick the family into which they will be born. Others hold that we know each other through many lifetimes and different incarnations. Whatever your belief system, have you ever felt so connected to another person that you felt you were soul mates? Did you ever meet someone for the first time and just instantly feel like you have known each other forever? Those are spiritual connections.

When a loved one dies, what is lost is the physical aspect of our relationship. We no longer get to see them, talk with them, hold them, or hear their voice. We tell ourselves that it's over. We have lost everything. But that's not true. We still are connected emotionally and spiritually. No matter what happens, we still have their loving spirit around us. We never have to lose the emotional or spiritual connections to our loved ones.

Think about the nature of the loss you are grieving. As you reflect on it, write your answers to the questions below.

1. For whom (or what) are you grieving?

    _____

    _____

    _____

    _____

2. When and how did your journey begin?

    _____

    _____

    _____

    _____

3. What were the physical aspects of the relationship that you enjoyed the most?

    _____

    _____

    _____

    _____

4. What were the emotional aspects of the relationship that you enjoyed the most?

    _____

    _____

    _____

    _____

5. What were the spiritual aspects of the relationship that you enjoyed the most?

    _____

    _____

    _____

    _____

6. How were the emotional aspects of the relationship different from the physical?

    _____

    _____

    _____

    _____

7. Which began first, the emotional or the physical part of the relationship? Which was most important?

_____

_____

_____

_____

8. What are your spiritual beliefs that pertain to this relationship?

_____

_____

_____

_____

9. Do you believe you will ever be together again?

_____

_____

_____

_____

10. What would this reunion be like for you?

_____

_____

_____

_____

11. How do you feel about the three aspects of your loss (physical, emotional, spiritual)? Does it make your grief more bearable to realize that you get to hold on to your emotional and spiritual connection even after your loss?

_____

_____

_____

_____

12. Make an inventory of your coping resources below. These may be people who will be emotionally supportive of your journey, places where you find peace and calm, things that comfort you, or activities that you find soothing or healing. If you list people, be sure to include their contact information.

1.
2.
3.
4.
5.
6.
7.
8.
9.
10.
11.
12.
13.
14.
15.
16.
17.
18.

19.

20.

The inventory you just made is crucial to your healing journey. It probably includes some items that may seem like luxuries, e.g., massage, or visits to the gym, or manicures. While you are recovering from a major loss these are not luxuries, rather they are things that can signal to your brain that it is possible to be happy again. It is possible to be fully engaged in your life again. Even going fishing, or walking your dog, or gardening, or listening to music can serve as reminders that you are still on the journey, there is more to come, and it will get better with time.

At the start of your journey you may have to push yourself to use your coping resources. It may feel like you are just going through the motions of life. But if you do use them and allow them to help you cope, you will come to a point when you are no longer merely coping, you are enjoying your life again.

As you recover it is important to protect yourself from further trauma if you can. Little things that you do can make a big difference, including making conscious choices about what you read, or watch on television or at the movies. This is not a good time to expose your self to violent action thrillers or horror movies. Anything that stimulates the monkey mind should be avoided or minimalized where possible. And, when you feel your self becoming agitated and those drunken monkeys are stirring around in your brain, use your coping resources to help restore a sense of calm and balance to your life.

This is one way to think about it: a major loss, like the death of a loved one, creates a catastrophic amount of stress in our life. Our brain is traumatized by the loss. We need to allow the brain the time it needs to heal and recover. We need to provide a loving, supportive environment to our self, just as the staff in a hospital would provide for us if we had a broken leg.

We need to make conscious choices about how we spend our time, whom we see, what we eat, and what we read or watch on television or the movies. To the extent that we can acknowledge our injury and provide an environment for ourselves to recover, we can hasten our return to a state of wellbeing.

Who Am I?

> *"At the center of your being you have the answer; you know who you are and you know what you want."*   Lao Tzu

THERE IS NOTHING like a major loss in life to cause us to seriously question our very existence. While we may have taken so many things for granted previously, the upsetting effect of any major shift, whether by a death, a professional setback, a divorce or other personal upheaval, causes us to second guess our very identity. The answer to the question "Who Am I?" becomes essential to finding our way back to equilibrium.

Here is a three-step exercise to help you go deeper into the essential nature of your identity. The best way to do this exercise is alone, and uninterrupted, preferably in a quiet place.

1. Who am I?

First, answer the question below in three different ways. But *none* of the three answers can be your actual name.

Who am I?

1. _____

2. _____

3. _____

We've been asking clients this simple question for twenty years at the Maui Transitions Center and we tend to get some pretty predictable results in the first part of this process.

When we eliminate the use of our name to answer the question, most clients resort to defining themselves in relation to other people or things. For example, they say things like, "I'm a mother," "I'm a husband," "I'm a parent of three children," "I'm a CEO of a company," or "I'm a lawyer," etc. In fact, we spend so much time self-identifying with objects, titles, or other relationships, we often forget that we are not those things; they are merely a part of our lives, a fraction of who we actually are.

II. Going Deeper

That is where the second step of the process comes in. Now I'm going to ask you to relax into a comfortable position and allow me to take you through a guided imagery. Just allow your mind to wander wherever the suggestion takes you. Don't evaluate. Just go with the imagery and trust the process.

With a little imagination and trust this process can be very beneficial to you. I'm going to give you the suggested prompts and after you read each one, just close your eyes and meditate on the words for a few minutes before going on to the next prompt. If you will slow down with this second step and be open to where your imagination may take you, you may have some surprising insights.

To begin, inhale slowly through your nose to a count of one, two, three, four. Then hold your breath to the same count of four. Then exhale slowly through your mouth to the same count of four.

Now do it again, even slower this time.

And do it yet again.

When we consciously slow down our breathing we are doing several things simultaneously. We are becoming mindful. We are reducing our stress levels. We are lowering our heart rate. We are signaling to our self that this is not just another unconscious breath among many millions we may take in a lifetime. This is different.

So when you have done at least three of these conscious breaths and are feeling more relaxed, slowly read through each of these guided imagery prompts and stay with whatever comes up for you through several more slow, deep breaths before you go on to the next prompt.

You have a name. You are *not* your name. Who are you?

(Take several slow, deep breaths as you think about your answer.)

You have a family. You are *not* your family. Who are you?

(Take several slow, deep breaths as you think about your answer.)

You have many relationships. You are *not* your relationships. Who are you?

(Take several slow, deep breaths as you think about your answer.)

You have an ego. You are *not* your ego. Who are you?

(Take several slow, deep breaths as you think about your answer.)

You have many possessions. These may include clothes, a house or apartment, a car, books, a boat, computers, shoes, pets, etc. You are *not* your possessions. Who are you?

(Take several slow, deep breaths as you think about your answer.)

You have a body. It may be strong and healthy. It may be old and weak. It may be thin, fat, muscular, tall, or short. You are *not* your body. Who are you?

(Take several slow, deep breaths as you think about your answer.)

You have a gender. You are *not* your gender. Who are you?

(Take several slow, deep breaths as you think about your answer.)

You may have a job or a title. You may have worked very hard to earn this position or this title. You are *not* your job or your title. Who are you?

(Take several slow, deep breaths as you think about your answer.)

You may have a religious belief. You may have held this belief for a very long time. You are *not* your religion. Who are you?

(Take several slow, deep breaths as you think about your answer.)

You have a national identity. You are *not* your national identity. Who are you?

(Take several slow, deep breaths as you think about your answer.)

You may have political beliefs. You may have held these beliefs for a very long time. You are *not* your political beliefs. Who are you?

(Take several slow, deep breaths as you think about your answer.)

You have a racial, or cultural identity. You are *not* your racial or cultural identity. Who are you?

(Take several deep breaths as you think about your answer.)

And now, free of the baggage of these labels, these external attributes, these artificial images of yourself, please use the space on the following page to either write or draw your answer to the essential question: Who am I?

Who Am I?

When I first did this exercise more than two decades ago, my answer to the question was not in words, but in a drawing. I drew golden light. It was meant to represent that I understood that in my core, in my essence, I am not a physical being at all. I am spirit. I am energy. I am light. You are, too.

We are taught from an early age that we are human beings. Actually, we are not. We are spiritual beings having a human experience, and probably not for the first time either.

At a scientific level of analysis, we are pure energy. Our bodies appear to be solid, but beneath that massive exterior is merely energy. Our atoms are moving so rapidly; they create the illusion of something that is solid. We buy into that illusion along with every other thing that comes with it, including the notion that we are different from other human beings based on external appearances, size, color, age, gender, etc. What a difference it would make in our life view if we truly understood that at our essence, where it matters, we are all alike. We are all vibrations of pure energy.

In Colorado we have blue skies most of the time, but occasionally some large clouds will roll through and bring afternoon thunderstorms or snow. Looking up at the sky as our big clouds are passing through we see a massive structure above us. Clouds can block the sun, lower the temperature, produce rain, sleet and snow, discharge energy through lightening and thunder, and even affect our moods or our plans for the day.

But clouds are deceptive. They look substantial and massive but all they really are, from a meteorological perspective, is an accumulation of water droplets and some chemicals hovering above the surface of the earth. They, like us, are transient, merely passing through. A cloud drops its rain or snow on us and then dissipates. It reforms again later when water is evaporated from the surface of the earth. We understand how irrational it would be to expect that clouds would always remain where we see them or that they would never change shape. But we fail to see how much like clouds our physical beings are. We can't hold onto a cloud, nor can we hold onto our physical shells. They may appear massive but it is all a misperception on our part.

1. Go outside today and spend some quiet time just watching clouds pass through the sky above. Can you see how our loved ones, and even we ourselves, are passing through as well? We change shape and dissipate, just like clouds. What insights do clouds offer for your grief process?

    _____

    _____

    _____

    _____

And how does the illusive nature of matter affect our ability to recover from major loss? The great genius Albert Einstein said that energy is neither created nor destroyed. It can only be changed from one form to another. If he is correct, then when a loved one dies, their energy still exists as a force in the world. We just relate to it differently. We can even think of it as the same essential life force or spirit that resides in each one of us. Loving spirit is simply loving the energy that we exude and that we experience as the essence of another. We can have a loving spirit. We can be a loving spirit. We can love the spirit that another person has or is.

Sometimes, especially when I'm writing, I can feel Allie's energy vibrating around me, especially when I get something wrong. It's like she stands over me and kind of edits my words as they go onto the page. It feels like a loving, positive force for good in my life and I welcome it. It helps me recover from her death if I can remind myself that she is still here, at least her energy is still here. And, since all I am is pure energy myself, we are both part of the same cosmic force field. My atoms may be simply vibrating at a different rate now than hers.

III. Reflection on spirit and loss

The final part of this exercise is a question for you to consider. How does a deeper understanding of who you are affect how you feel about the loss in your life?

_____

_____

_____

_____

What is Grief?

"If you are depressed you are living in the past. If you are anxious you are living in the future. If you are at peace you are living in the present."
Lao Tzu

GRIEF IS A good thing.

Grief is a healthy human response to loss. If someone cuts us, we bleed. If we break a leg, we go see a doctor. If we lose someone or something we love, we grieve.

It really ought to be that simple. But usually it's not. It gets complicated by our strong emotions, it gets denied, it gets stigmatized, it gets delayed by other distractions, it gets compounded by other losses piling on over time, it gets sermonized by all kinds of religious beliefs, and it gets avoided because it can be quite messy and embarrassing.

There is an important physiological aspect to grief that is often overlooked. Our inability or refusal to confront the emotions that grief generates results in predictable physiological manifestations of symptoms and even illness. If we consciously suppress our feelings of grief, due to family pressures or social constraints, the effect of that suppression can be later experienced as irritability, mood swings, tension in the neck and back, headaches, muscle cramps, menstrual disorders, colitis, indigestion, insomnia, hypertension, allergies, and more, according to medical studies. See, "Letting Go: The Pathway of Surrender," David R. Hawkins, M.D., Ph.D.

So you might be thinking, that if suppression causes all these problems then expression of our angst, or anger toward whomever caused us to feel badly would be the better approach. And you'd be wrong, at least according to Sigmund Freud, the father of psychoanalysis. Instead of expressing our frustration against any offender, the better course is to neutralize the negativity by channeling it into constructive forces of love, work and creativity.

The Diagnostic and Statistical Manual of Mental Disorders, calls grief a "catastrophic stressor." Given that about 2.5 million Americans died in 2010, that means that a lot of us are carrying around a huge amount of stress as a consequence of grief. And, if we don't learn how to have healthier responses to grief, this high stress level could lead to our own illnesses, hospitalizations, and even more deaths.

In *Life After Loss*, Dr. Vamik Volkan and Elizabeth Zintl define the grief that we experience immediately after the loss as "crisis grief." This is the time during which our response shifts from denial to acceptance. In the immediate aftermath of Allie's death, I exhibited many symptoms of crisis grief.

In the 1:00 a.m. phone call when the doctor told me that Allie had been found non-responsive, I couldn't even respond. I just started shaking my head in disbelief. And when he called back three hours later to tell me she had just been pronounced dead, I left the beach house where we were staying and walked along the shore in a dense fog just screaming and screaming. I didn't even realize that I was screaming. For two years thereafter my sleep patterns were disturbed. I would awaken at 1:00 a.m. and not be able to go back to sleep again until after 4:30 a.m. I obsessively replayed the conversation in my brain trying desperately to alter the outcome.

It was a time of excessive agitation, and compulsive eating. Do you know how irritating it is to have something in your eye but you can't see it? Every blink causes a level of pain and irritation that feels like it shoots directly into your brain. It is so invasive that it becomes impossible to think about or to do anything else except try to get it out. You rub your eye incessantly, probably making matters worse. It becomes red, irritated, and tears start to fall. Arrrrggggghhhh! That is similar to the level of excessive agitation that accompanied the crisis grief stage for me.

Excessive agitation and compulsive eating are not my normal states of being. But for the first couple of years they were all I could muster as a response to Allie's death. I knew that I was behaving obsessively, but self-awareness wasn't enough to change the behavior or reduce the level of my agitation, especially in the stage of crisis grief.

The chart below shows the many ways grief can negatively impact our lives. This data was drawn from many medical research articles.

MANIFESTATIONS
OF
GRIEF

EMOTIONAL RESPONSES
- SADNESS
- YEARNING
- ANXIETY
- GUILT
- IRRITABILITY
- NUMBNESS
- DETACHMENT
- CONFUSION
- SHOCK
- ANGER
- DISBELIEF
- WORRY
- LONELINESS

PHYSIOLOGICAL RESPONSES
- DIGESTIVE UPSET
- FATIGUE/EXHAUSTION
- HEADACHES
- CHEST PAINS
- SORE MUSCLES
- SLEEP DIFFICULTIES
- POOR APPETITE/OVEREATING
- SHAKINESS/TREMBLING
- IMPULSIVITY
- LOST SEXUAL DESIRE/HYPER SEXUALITY
- CRYING
- SIGHING
- HEAVINESS

BEHAVIORAL RESPONSES
- RESTLESSNESS
- SOCIAL WITHDRAWAL
- ABSENTMINDNESS
- INABILITY TO CONCENTRATE
- HYPER ACTIVE

HEALTH RESPONSES
- CORTISOL ELEVATION
- LOWER IMMUNITY
- HEART RATE
- BLOOD PRESSURE
- CARDIAC RISK
- THROMBIC
- INCREASED MORTALITY

SURREAL WORLD RESPONSES
- DREAM-LIKE
- FLOATING
- TIME BLURS
- DISASSOCIATION
- IT DIDN'T HAPPEN

In my own period of crisis grief I suffered from thirty of these effects of grief. There were possibly more that affected me of which I was unaware.

1. Think about your own grief experience. What were/are the symptoms of your crisis response to your loss, e.g., feelings or behaviors?

    _____

    _____

    _____

    _____

2. Were some of your behaviors that allowed you to initially cope with your overwhelming feelings of loss actually things that were bad for you? Be specific about anything you did that was not a healthy response, e.g., drinking or over eating, etc.

    _____

    _____

    _____

    _____

3. If so, how did your response shift or change over time?

    _____

    _____

    _____

    _____

One of the best ways to help us recover from grief is to learn how to reduce our stress levels. This can take many forms, including:

exercise, sports, meditation, prayer, yoga, crossword puzzles, reading, being in nature, talking with a friend or advisor, etc. Men and women seem to elect different paths to reduce their stress levels. There is no right or wrong here, merely different preferences. Choose the path that feels right to you.

4. What efforts have you made to reduce your stress levels since your loss? (If a truthful answer is none, list efforts you could undertake.)

    _____

    _____

    _____

    _____

Dr. Volkan and Ms. Zintl make the point that crisis grief ends when we are no longer stuck in denial. The full reality of what we have lost is accepted, and although we don't like it, we at least learn to live with it. I don't know when I stopped expecting Allie to call me, or when I no longer thought of calling her. Nor can I say exactly when I fully internalized just how complete the loss was. Sometime between day one of my journey and the end of year two, I slowly came to be at peace with reality. The reality was that she was dead. Life was simply different now. I had to face that and go on.

5. Are you still in crisis grief, or have you moved beyond that stage?

    _____

6. What were/are the symptoms of your crisis response to your loss?

    _____

    _____

    _____

    _____

When I was no longer in the crisis stage of grief, a general kind of melancholy set in. I wasn't crying every day, but I wasn't smiling or laughing either. I made it through daily activities and continued to work with clients, but on some level a part of me was missing. I was less than fully present. My body was showing up but my heart was absent. I was on a kind of automatic pilot setting, technically flying the plane, but almost completely removed from an awareness of what was happening around me.

In an effort to understand what was happening to me I began to read more about grief and recovery. I searched online and in bookstores for wisdom. That's when I discovered the work of David Hawkins, M.D., Ph.D.

Dr. Hawkins spent twenty years studying levels of human consciousness through the use of behavioral kinesiology correlated with a logarithmic scale to calibrate the relative power of the energy of different thoughts and attitudes. I hadn't known that even our thoughts and attitudes have energy. All I knew was that I was in the pits. I just wasn't functioning at my usual level of capacity and it felt like I was stuck in a rut.

Based on millions of calibrations on thousands of test subjects of all ages, backgrounds, and personality types, Dr. Hawkins was able to calibrate that consciousness has an energy vibrational level of 200. Mere physical existence is calibrated at 1. Levels of love and joy are in the range of 500 and 540, respectively. I simply was not being very conscious in this phase of my grief process and I was certainly not feeling love and joy in my life.

In his phenomenal best seller, *Power vs. Force*, Dr. Hawkins makes the compelling point that grief is actually an unconscious state of being. Its energy vibration is calibrated at a level of only 75. He calls it the "cemetery of life." Its hallmarks are having a life view that is tragic and being filled with regret and despondency. Victimhood calibrates at an even lower level of 40.

I didn't read *Power vs. Force*, until after Allie died. For a long time I couldn't concentrate long enough to finish a newspaper article. But when I began reading again I was drawn to this book almost magnetically. I needed to read it and somehow it found me and pulled me in. I'm very glad that happened because after reading it I realized that I absolutely couldn't stay in grief. Whatever it took, any amount of self-discipline, therapy, spiritual practice, or by any other means required, I had to unslump myself.

Although it was impossible not to feel grief for the loss of my beloved daughter, I knew that I couldn't allow myself to stay in that state for long or else it would kill me.

Dr. Hawkins described it this way: "Grief is the level of sadness, loss, and despondency. Most of us have experienced it for periods of time, but those who remain at this level live a life of constant regret and depression. This is the level of mourning, bereavement, and remorse about the past; it's also the level of habitual losers and those chronic gamblers who accept failure as part of their lifestyle, often resulting in loss of jobs, friends, family and opportunity, as well as money and health."

This was a huge wake-up call for me.

So I looked at the rest of his book to see what tools could I use to help lift me out of a state of grief. They included some bedrock character traits, like courage, affirmation, empowerment, hope, optimism, forgiveness and acceptance. These were things I could focus on, practice, and learn from.

I began meditating, starting each day by reading runes for inspiration, expressing appreciation more frequently and more thoughtfully, and showing more compassion for those less fortunate. These practices got me to start thinking more about others and less about myself.

In the back of my mind, little phrases kept repeating as mantras, like "this too, shall pass," "not my will but Thine be done," and "I surrender all."

Little by little, I could feel my mood lightening. There were some days when it was all gloom and doom again, but they became fewer over time and the good days began to outnumber the bad. After about two years of grief I would say that I no longer carried that hole in my heart. I had scar tissue, for sure, but scar tissue is a good thing.

7. What steps are you taking to help yourself move beyond a state of grief? If a truthful answer is "none," list the steps you could or should take.

_____

_____

_____

_____

Here's the really good news. Every little step you take makes a logarithmic difference in your consciousness, not just an arithmetic difference. Grief vibrates at 75, Anger at 150. But anger isn't merely twice the vibrational level of grief it is 10 to the 150th power higher. For those of us who are not mathematically inclined, just think of it as being a gazillion times better.

Getting in touch with our anger can actually help lessen our grief, as can forgiveness and acceptance. While it's important to be conscious of our angry feelings, it's equally important not to vent them toward anyone else. There are more constructive ways to resolve angry emotions than yelling at your family members. We will explore ways to do these things more effectively in the coming chapters.

What Has Been My Journey?

"Your own positive future begins in this moment. All you have is right now. Every goal is possible from here."   Lao Tzu

MOST PEOPLE REACH out for help when they are in pain. If you bought this book, or checked it out from a library, you are probably experiencing a difficult time in your life. You may even be feeling that it will never get better. I can assure you that this, too, will pass. I can even share a little secret with you that you may not know yet. This is it: you are stronger than you realize.

How do I know?

On my left arm there is a rather sizable scar and an indentation where skin and muscle tissue used to be. It is the site of a small surgery that I had to remove a basal cell carcinoma. It's not pretty to look at, but it actually makes me feel kind of proud when I see it. That's because scar tissue does not form on dead bodies. So the fact that I have a scar at all means that I survived skin cancer. Scar tissue is made of collagen. Because it is fibrous, it is actually stronger than the skin around it. My scar reminds me that I am stronger now in the very spot where I once was most vulnerable. I only have to glance at my arm to feel better about where life has taken me since that basal cell was diagnosed.

Four years ago, when Allie died, it left me with new scar tissue. My heart was broken. My spirit was slumped. My outlook on life was pretty bleak. I had quite a few new mental and emotional scars from the loss. And, I've been working pretty hard ever since to heal them. You are probably in a similar place, too.

The purpose of this next exercise is to remind ourselves that the wound that feels so painful to us right now is not the first wounding experience we've had, nor will it likely be the last. But if we can look back on our lives from the beginning until now, we will see that along the way we have experienced some life-changing events and learned quite a few lessons from our journey to date. Taking the time to review our life so far helps us put the current loss or difficulty in perspective. Or even if the thing we are now challenged by is actually the worst thing that has ever happened to us, we can still learn from it and grow beyond it.

1. You are now going to create a lifeline. It is a personal account of the major events in your life to date, both positive and negative. Beginning from birth, until the present time, list on the left side of the ledger below the major negative events in your life to date. Use short words or even abbreviations to remind you of the event. On the right side list the positive events. Even a young adult will have several entries on each side of the ledger. Don't worry about specific dates; just try to get within the five year time span if you can't remember exactly when a major event happened.

Use the chart that follows for your lifeline.

Negative Events   **Positive Events**

Birth

5 Years Old

10 Years Old

15 Years Old

20 Years Old

25 Years Old

30 Years Old

35 Years Old

40 Years Old

45 Years Old

50 Years Old

55 Years Old

60 Years Old

65 Years Old

Over 70 Years Old

2. Looking back over your life in perspective, what would you say have been the most important events, both positive and negative, that have occurred so far?

_____

_____

_____

_____

_____

_____

3. As you review your life to date, what lessons have you learned from either the positive or negative events?

_____

_____

_____

_____

_____

_____

4. Based on what you have learned so far, what advice would you give to someone in your current situation?

_____

_____

_____

_____

_____

_____

5. Are you listening to your own inner wisdom in your current situation? If not, why not?

_____

_____

_____

_____

_____

_____

Sometimes when life's losses are so disruptive to our sense of normalcy it helps to begin again, with the end in mind. And of course, the ultimate end is our own death.

The next exercise is intended to help you realize what the consequences would be if your life ended today. Would there be things that were important that you meant to do? Were there relationships that needed tending? What was your life's essential meaning? How would you want to be remembered?

6. For this exercise, imagine that you died today. Use the space below and on the next page to write your own obituary, as you would want it to appear in a national newspaper.

_____

_____

_____

_____

_____

_____

_____

_____

_____

_____

_____

_____

_____

_____

_____

_____

_____

_____

_____

_____

7.   Now that you have imagined your own death and its consequences, make a list of things you need to do before you actually die in order to feel at peace with the life you have led. Add to the list any things you would want to enjoy as well.

1.
2.
3.
4.
5.
6.
7.
8.
9.
10.
11.
12.
13.
14.
15.
16.
17.
18.
19.
20.

The list above now becomes your to-do list. If you feel depressed and don't want to face the day, look back on this list to see if you have completed all the items you wrote. If not, get on it! After all, death is certain. The timing is not. You may not have any time to waste.

What is My Type?

"Knowing others is Wisdom, knowing yourself is Enlightenment."
Lao Tzu

FOR THE PAST twenty years, I've been using a very beneficial tool to help clients understand themselves more deeply. It is called the Myers-Briggs Type Indicator (MBTI). It is based on the writings of Carl Jung, the father of analytical psychology. The MBTI is one of hundreds of tools that are available to help us understand each other more deeply. I like it because it allows me to be direct with clients about things they are doing that sabotage their own progress without wounding them. It helps create an environment to honestly talk about our differences in non-judgmental terms.

Normally, in a workshop I would spend about four hours just explaining the basics of type and its proper usage. What follows in this chapter and the next is a brief introduction to the subject and then a specific look at how it impacts the way we grieve. In my opinion, if there were a deeper understanding of these dynamics there would be fewer divorces following major losses. We'd be able to talk about why we react differently to traumatic situations without playing the blame game. I believe that a better understanding of our personality types could help reduce the bereavement-related divorce numbers.

These two chapters will be better understood if you have actually taken a Myers-Briggs Type Indicator assessment. I have made them accessible on my website: www.daylespencer.com/mbti for a nominal charge. When you take the assessment you will receive a personalized report of your personality type that can be a real asset to you as you navigate the journey of loss.

My strong advice is that you go to the website now, complete the assessment and then read the next two chapters when you have received your personalized results. The results are sent within 24 hours of completion of the online assessment. The assessment usually takes about thirty minutes to complete.

(Note to reader: if you do not know your MBTI type or do not wish to take the assessment at this time, you may want to skip over these two chapters for now.)

In the 1920s, Carl Jung began describing how our personalities develop from the moment of birth. The preferences we express for certain fundamental aspects of our personalities influence whether we get our energy from external events and other people (Extraversion), or whether we energize by being alone and quiet with our thoughts for company (Introversion).

They impact our choice for what kind of information we rely upon in the most important affairs in our life too, whether we want to see tangible proof (Sensing), or prefer to trust our inner way of knowing (iNtuition). (We use a capital N in spelling iNtuition in type talk because we have already used a capital I to represent the world of Introversion.)

We also make decisions based on whether we have a preference for doing it objectively, in a kind of depersonalized way (Thinking), or we take individual circumstances into account in a subjective way (Feeling). This is not to suggest that Thinkers don't feel, or that Feelers don't think. Of course they do! Rather, when it comes to how each will decide a given issue, one type will use objective criteria (policy, rules, laws, etc.) and the other type will use subjective criteria (fairness, personal knowledge, individual circumstances, etc.).

And finally, the MBTI shows us how we prefer to live our lives, whether we like a world that is orderly, structured, planned (Judging), or one that is flexible, spontaneous and easygoing (Perceiving). Judgers have opinions about almost everything, and they don't like surprises. Perceivers don't care as much about the outcome as they do about the process being fair, and they don't like to be fenced in.

You may well ask if Jung came up with these archetypes, then why is it called the Myers-Briggs Type Indicator? Katharine Briggs and her daughter Isabel Briggs Myers began to work with the notion of quantifying Jung's theories about the development of our personality preferences and making them more easily understood by a wide audience. They developed the tool of the MBTI in the 1940s. The research has been ongoing ever since its introduction. Their tool allows us to visually understand Jung's classifications of preferences and to think of individuals as being one of sixteen types, with all types being of equal value.

Millions of people have now taken the assessment, which is currently offered in twenty-one languages. It has become such a reliable and effective tool for my work that I will no longer work with a client who is unwilling to look closely at his or her personality type.

Will and I like this particular tool so much that when either of our sons brings home someone they are serious about to meet us for the first time, we offer the potential new daughter-in-law an MBTI assessment to help strengthen the bond between them. I have sat down with the couple and explained how their particular types might get into disagreements, where they might be very compatible, and how they look, compared to the rest of our family. We have probably frightened a couple of them away by doing this, if the truth were told.

For purposes of using this tool to help you recover from a major loss in life, consider the following. On a good day, you get to operate in your preferred world making decisions your way, trusting information that seems reliable to you, either engaging others in the world or not, and making your plans and orderly decisions, or keeping your options open, depending on your preferences. Most of the time we operate in our preferred environment and we feel safe, confident, and at ease.

That's not to suggest that we can't be effective even if we have to function out of our preferences. We've had presidents of the United

States who were introverts. They could rise to the challenge of public speaking, meeting lots of strangers, and life in the ultimate fishbowl by balancing the needs of their profession with their personal style. Probably when they retreated upstairs at the White House at night, it was to a quieter cocoon-like environment that allowed them to renew their energies. We've also had presidents who were such clear extraverts that after a full day of meetings, public functions, and pressing the flesh, they stayed on the telephone most of the night lobbying Congress or other world leaders and renewing their energy in this extraverted way long after most of their staff had gone to bed. But even the clearest extravert can be quite happy to curl up with a good book and read quietly, occasionally.

Taking the MBTI assessment allows us to have an objective way of looking at our self and seeing more deeply into our true nature. If you look at your two-page report you will notice that on the first page it shows your type in colored blocks of letters. You are either E or I, S or N, T or F, J or P. Four of these possible type-combinations will be highlighted in blue on your report. So, for example, if you are like me, and are an Extraverted, iNtuitive, Feeling, Perceiver, the letters ENFP will be in blue on page one of your report.

1. Based on your report, what is your type? (Give the letter and the preference for each of the four aspects of your type, e.g., E, Extraversion).

    _____

2. When you read the description of your reported type on page one, did you agree with the assessment? Why or why not?

    _____

    _____

    _____

    Take a look at page two of your report.

The graph at the top shows how clearly you prefer one way of being over its opposite. If you scored in the very clear range numerically, 25-30, (i.e., have a long bar on either side of the graph) you are someone who is really comfortable doing things that certain way. A person who has only slight scores (0-5) might easily adapt to the other way of being, depending on the circumstances they are facing.

You might have scored from 1-30 as an extravert, or a person who is not like you, might have scored from 1-30 as an introvert. If you two are total opposites, you may have scored a 30 on one scale while your opposite type scored a 30 on the opposite scale.

3. Record below both the letter preference and numerical score (the qualitative and quantitative assessments) for your type. (Example, E=25, N=14, etc.).

_____

_____

_____

At the bottom of page two of your report, there is a chart showing all of the sixteen possible type combinations. Your type is highlighted in yellow. You are also given a brief description of the typical personality traits of someone like you.

The first time I took the MBTI assessment, I read about my type and the aspects of my personality and it seemed to me that someone finally understood me. Most people report that the assessment accurately captures the essence of who they are. But there is no instrument that can precisely predict all the complexities of human behaviors. This one gives us some useful descriptors and a place to start a conversation about difficult issues.

4. Now look at the chart below. This chart shows the sixteen personality types and, with a percentage amount, tells you

how often your type occurs in the general population. It also has an underline that reflects the dominant function of your personality. Pay attention to the underlined function, as it will become important as we focus on how we grieve.

Ideally, for a grieving family, we would assess the types of the whole group so that as they move through the journey of grief and recovery, each person would have an awareness of why they might respond to issues or circumstances differently than the rest of the family. It can help avoid major rifts, especially in highly stressful situations like grief, or divorce or other major life change.

5. Circle your type in the chart that follows and make note of your dominant function in the space provided. We will discuss this more in the following chapter. (For example, my type, ENFP, has the dominant function of intuition.)

TYPE PREVALENCE AND DOMINANT FUNCTION

I<u>S</u>TJ 6%	I<u>S</u>FJ 6%	I<u>N</u>FJ 1%	I<u>N</u>TJ 1%
IS<u>T</u>P 5%	IS<u>F</u>P 5%	IN<u>F</u>P 1%	IN<u>T</u>P 1%
ES<u>T</u>P 13%	ES<u>F</u>P 13%	E<u>N</u>FP 5%	E<u>N</u>TP 5%
ES<u>T</u>J 13%	ES<u>F</u>J 15%	EN<u>F</u>J 5%	EN<u>T</u>J 5%

6. My type's dominant function is:

_____

In the next Chapter we will examine the implications for how your type experiences grief differently from others.

How Does My Type Grieve?

"When you are at one with loss, the loss is experienced willingly."
Lao Tzu

ROBABLY THE MOST honest answer to the question of how people grieve is that we grieve as best we can for as long as it takes. It's usually not a pretty process. And at times we may feel hopelessly lost just wondering if there is anything else we could do, or something we could do differently to make it better. Worse, we compare our response to others who have also suffered a loss and think that we are doing it all wrong. You may be doing it differently, but that doesn't make it wrong.

We respond to grief and other major losses in fairly predictable ways that have everything to do with our personality types. Of course family history, culture, religion, and traditions also play a role, but for now, let's look at how our personalities influence how we grieve.

1. First, look back at your MBTI report and remind yourself of your type. (The four letter combination will do for now.)

Extraverts and Introverts

You are either an extravert or an introvert. This is the first letter of your type. Remember extraverts get energized externally, by being with other people. Introverts go within to renew their energy.

This would suggest that whenever something goes wrong in their lives, the extraverted response would be to want to talk about it. Extraverts feel comfortable venting their feelings to others. They enjoy group meetings and group activities. So an extravert is likely to join a support group of Compassionate Friends, or a church group of mourners. The extraverted griever may also benefit from working with a therapist with whom they could talk on a regular, confidential basis. Having the company and the support of others would be a beneficial thing for extraverts, and the more clearly they have this preference (the longer the first bar on the graph on page two of the report), the more they will need other folks around them as they grieve.

Introverts are not like that. Introverts process events internally. They tend to think before they speak about their thoughts or feelings. An introvert may not welcome a public funeral, or a wake, or any sort of large gathering in a time of loss, preferring instead to seek their own, internal solace and guidance. As with extraverts, the longer the first bar on the graph on page two of the report, the more likely the introverted response would be to seek solitude, quiet and reflection, rather than group gatherings.

If an introverted griever needs support he or she might first seek answers in books before turning to therapists or support groups. Rather than talking about his or her feelings, an introvert might prefer to write about them, journaling as the grief process continues. And when an introvert does reach out to others for help, it is likely to be with only one or two trusted friends or advisors.

1. Look back at page two of your MBTI report. Notice the first line on the bar graph and how clear your preference is for either extraversion or introversion. As you think about your journey of loss and the way you have responded to it so far, would you say you have acted in ways that are typical for your type, or not? If not, how have your responses been different?

_____

_____

_____

_____

Remember, no instrument or assessment can accurately predict all the variables of human behaviors. This one is a good framework to allow us to be open with each other about important differences in style.

Judgers and Perceivers

Now, let's look at the bottom line of the graph on page two of your report. This shows our preferences for how we like to live our lives. This is the difference between those who are judgers and those who are perceivers.

A judger likes a well-planned, organized, decided, settled life. They do not like surprises. They do not like feeling out of control. Judgers tend to run our school systems and very tight ships.

A perceiver, on the other hand, feels stifled when things are too orderly. They need spontaneity, freedom, and keeping their options open. Perceivers probably invented the term hang loose, as that is what they enjoy.

With an image of these two life styles in mind, add to the mix that someone they love has just died. Can you imagine anything more threatening to a judger's world than the feeling of being out of control this would bring? Especially if the death were sudden, unexpected, or even violent, a judger would feel that the world they knew (and preferred) has been changed forever.

For perceivers, the sudden loss of a loved one is an equally tragic event, however their response might be different. Because they are fundamentally the kind of go-with-the-flow people, even this drastic change in the flow would likely pose less of a threat for them than their judging friends and families. Where perceivers might get hung up is on the unfairness of how the death might have occurred. A perceiver who thinks the process is fair can usually accept the outcome. Perceivers are cat-like. They land on their feet.

2. Look back at page two of your MBTI report. Notice the last line on the bar graph and how clear your preference is for either judging or perceiving. As you think about your journey of loss and the way you have responded to it so far, would you say you have acted in ways that are typical for your type, or not? If not, how have your responses been different?

_____

_____

_____

_____

Remember, if you have slight scores on any of the four scales, you may look more like the other type at times. Overall, you have a slight preference for the one that is shown as your type.

Why Does This Matter?

Let's go back to our friend Carl Jung, who started all this almost one hundred years ago. Jung said that when we are under stress we don't act like our normal selves. (Duh, right?) In fact, under stress we act like the extreme opposite of our normal selves.

I think of this as being like the character Jim Carrey played in *The Mask*. Whenever his character put on the mask he became an out of control, berserk, animated creature literally bouncing off the walls. That kind of flailing was exactly how I felt during the period of crisis grief immediately after Allie died. Maybe you have felt it, too.

Now, I want you to go back to last page of the previous chapter and the chart that had an underline below one of the letters of your type. I had you write down the dominant function of your personality (it was underlined) as the last exercise in that chapter.

It is really helpful to know what our dominant function is because that is the strongest, most reliable part of our personality. Jung said we begin to develop this function by about age six and we rely on it in the most important of our daily affairs.

If yours happens to be sensing, it means that since you were just a child you have wanted to know the facts, you were in touch with reality. You trusted things that could be proven. If yours is intuition, on the other hand, it means that you have always had a kind of sixth sense that you relied on. You may have also had a great imagination and liked to pretend. If your dominant function is thinking, it means that even as a child you looked for logical explanations of things, you were objective and decided things based on rules. And, finally, if your dominant function is feeling, you were always trying to help everyone get along and you decided things on the basis of what was fair.

So, there you are, rocking along, using your dominant function to help guide your path since age six, and then someone you love dies, or you have any other major setback, like a divorce, or career change, or change in the meaning, identity or structure of your life.

What do you do? Well you might think that since you have trusted and relied on your dominant function for so long, and it has served you so well, that you would simply use it to solve whatever problem life presented, right?

Wrong.

In times of high stress, e.g., a catastrophic stressor like the death of a loved one, we don't lead with what we know best. We lead with the least developed, least preferred part of our personality. We lead with what is called our inferior function. It is the opposite of our dominant function, and, like Jim Carrey's character in *The Mask*, it can make us look pretty foolish at times.

We even call our inferior function our Achilles' heel, because it is so vulnerable. So, you are probably asking yourself by now, what is my inferior function? Where am I most vulnerable under times of stress?

3. Remember the dominant function from the previous chapter? If yours was sensing, then your inferior function is intuition. If yours was thinking, then your inferior function is feeling, and vice versa.

What is my inferior function?

_____

You already know that my MBTI Type is E (Extraverted), N (iNtuitive), F (Feeling), P (Perceiving). My dominant function is intuition. I'm a big picture person, I like to use my imagination, and I trust my inner ways of knowing whether something is true or right for me. So if intuition is my dominant function, then my inferior function is the opposite of that, or sensing. Sensing is how I get into trouble when I'm stressed out.

If you are like me, and have sensing as your inferior function, beware. Under stress, out of fear, we start engaging the world through an immature, out of control, sensing lens. We can obsess about the smallest fact or detail and refuse to let it go. We can overeat. We can start drinking or smoking, or using drugs (these are all sensory experiences taken to extreme, right?).

What happened for me years ago when my mother had a stroke was that I became obsessed with researching what causes strokes, how to treat them, what medicines work and don't work. I was literally staying up late at night reading the *Physician's Desk Reference* on prescription medicines so I would understand all the possible drug interactions. It was nuts. I was nuts. I was in my shadow. The shadow side of our personality is the part of us that we are embarrassed by, don't have good control over, and usually refuse to acknowledge even exists within us. But it is also the first thing that we criticize when we see it displayed in others.

When Allie died, I started eating pints of Haagen-Dazs on a regular basis. The freezer always had at least one and sometimes two on hand. I ate so much of it that I gained forty pounds. Since my husband Will's Type is INTJ, it means that although we are very different, we share the same inferior function. We both gained about the same amount of excess weight as we grieved. Not smart, right? I knew better. I even knew from a psychological perspective what I was doing and why, but I couldn't stop myself for a long time. Now I'm on a diet and am losing the weight. But I'm able to do that because I'm in a much less stressful state now.

When our inferior function gets out of control, we need to shift the pendulum back to our dominant function to be back in charge of our lives. For me, with intuition as my dominant function, that meant asking myself: "What's the big picture here?" and "Where do I want to be in a year or two?" If I didn't want to become diabetic, I knew I had to stop eating all the ice cream. And gradually, I did.

Here is a summary of how the sixteen types act or look under great stress. Find your type in it and read its description. And as you do, be aware that other members of your family will likely have different, and even opposite types. So read all the descriptions, but pay particular attention to your own type under great stress.

If your type is, ISTJ, ISFJ, ESTP, or ESFP, then your inferior function is intuition. Under stress your intuition may run amok. You may start seeing patterns or connections where none really exist. You may see the future in negative terms, be unduly pessimistic, get stuck and not see possible ways out, or get caught in a rut. If you are extraverted as well, you may become withdrawn, impractical, delusional, or self-depreciating. If you are introverted as well, you may become impulsive, paranoid, fearful or suspicious.

If your type is, INFJ, INTJ, ENFP, or ENTP, then your inferior function is sensing. Under stress what you take in through your five senses may run amok. You may either disregard or overly rely on facts, or take in sensual stimuli (overeating, gulping food or alcohol, smoking incessantly, etc.) in an out of control way. You may even exercise compulsively. If you are also extraverted, you may become withdrawn, grumpy, or physically ill. If, on the other hand, you are introverted, you may become adversarial or obsess about the smallest details.

If your type is, INTP, ISTP, ENTJ, or ESTJ, then your inferior function is feeling. Under stress your feelings may run amok. You can become overwhelmed or over-zealous. You may have uncontrolled emotional outbursts, show anger or other emotions unexpectedly, be hypersensitive, or take criticism very personally. And If you are extraverted, you may become unruly, or inappropriately loving or hateful, or illogical. However, if you are introverted, you may become explosive, illogical, or even fanatical.

If your type is, ISFP, INFP, ESFJ, or ENFJ, then your inferior function is thinking. Under stress your objectivity runs amok. You can become inflexible, even rigid. You may be hypercritical, finding fault with almost everything. You may be overly domineering, taking charge without listening to others. If you are extraverted, you may withdraw, or become melancholic, or caustic. If you are introverted, you may become domineering, loud or even tyrannical.

Is it any wonder that families fight while grieving? Imagine the perfect storm, that someone whose inferior function is thinking (either an ISFP, INFP, ESFJ, or an ENFJ) suddenly decides to take charge of all the funeral arrangements and makes critical decisions that impact the entire family without listening to others' input. And, when anyone else tries to help they can only criticize the efforts of others. Combine this type of person under stress, with a family member whose inferior function is just the opposite, feeling (either an ISTP, INTP, ESTJ, or an ENTJ), and you will get a hypersensitive person feeling bulldozed by a hypercritical person who won't listen.

Both are functioning from the least mature parts of their personalities and each can inflict terrible wounds on the other without even realizing the damage is being done until it is too late. Given that the immature feeler is likely to have uncontrolled emotional outbursts, it is easy to see how families can actually come to blows or end up not speaking to other family members thereafter, when a loved one suddenly dies. It takes a tremendous amount of emotional restraint to realize this dynamic is happening and to step back from the escalating tensions before the damage becomes irreparable.

So, how can anyone avoid running amok, or being in their shadow, in times of great emotional stress? One of the simplest ways is to recognize the symptoms of stress that you manifest before they build to the point of explosion. Does your pulse rate increase? Do you feel your anger rising? Are you aware of your breath becoming more rapid and shallow? When you become aware of the increasing pressure build up, learn to consciously assess your dominant function to help you avoid a meltdown.

For those whose dominant function is thinking, you can ask yourself, "What's happening here, objectively?" "What would be the logical thing to do?" and "What do I think the right outcome should be?" These kinds of logical, rational questions allow a dominant thinker to assess his or her greatest strength to solve a crisis.

For those whose dominant function is feeling, on the other hand, questions like: "What would be the fair thing to do?" "How can we find a solution that would create more harmony for everyone?" and "Is there a win/win here?" can also allow you to use your strength to resolve confrontations.

For those whose dominant function is sensing, you can ask yourself: "What are the facts?" "What is realistic in this situation?" and "What's been tried before, and how did it work?" This kind of inquiry results in data that will feel solid and reliable to a sensor even under stress.

And, for those whose dominant function is intuition, on the other hand, questions like: "What's the big picture here?" "What are some possibilities that haven't been tried yet?" and "What path would serve us best in the future?" allow the use of the greatest strength of your type.

If you can just take several slow deep breaths, before engaging, and delay long enough to remember what your dominant function is and to ask yourself these kinds of critical questions, the escalation of many crises can be avoided. A few seconds spent in conscious breathing and remembering the greatest strength of our personality can help us begin to avoid the landmines that litter the paths of emotionally charged situations and relationships.

4. Find the description of your type in shadow above. Based on what you read answer the following questions.

   Have you been experiencing behaviors that are described above for your type? If so, describe a specific incident when your behavior was out of control and/or not at all like your normal self.

   _____

   _____

   _____

   _____

5. If you are one of those readers who is now having an "Aha!" moment because you realize that under stress you behaved badly, it isn't too late. You can apologize, ask for forgiveness, or make amends. To whom do you need to apologize for your behavior when you ran amok?

   1.
   2.
   3.
   4.
   5.

   Grief is a time of exhaustion. Our batteries are seriously drained and not much time is spent replenishing our emotional banks. A kind of chronic fatigue can set in. We may even develop a physical illness. I developed shingles, which is an excruciatingly painful viral infection. These physiological manifestations of grief are nature's way of reminding us to take better care of ourselves and to pay attention to our bodies and our physical needs.

When we look back on our journey we realize that even at our worst there were some valuable lessons learned from the experience, although they came at a price. The shadow side of our personality offers us wisdom that can only be gleaned from being in the darkness. The challenge is not to let the dark times overwhelm us, or sabotage our relationships.

6. Thinking back on times of your greatest stress, when you felt like your inferior function was running amok, what lessons would you say you learned?

_____

_____

_____

_____

7. Now that you know just how badly catastrophic stress can impact your personality and even your overall heath, what precautions can you take to avoid shadow behaviors?

1.

2.

3.

4.

5.

6.

7.

8.

9.

10.

What Do I Believe?

*"A man with outward courage dares to die; a man with inner
courage dares to live."* Lao Tzu, *Tao Te Ching*

ONE OF OUR dear friends is a lifelong Christian, a deacon
in his church, and someone whom I respect as a person who walks
his talk. But a few years ago, after his daughter died at aged 40 from
brain cancer, leaving behind a husband and two boys, my friend lost
his faith in God. He did not believe that a just and loving God could
have put his child through such suffering and then take her from
them so early in life and in such a brutal way. He stopped praying
and he stopped going to church after her funeral.

On the other hand, one of our clients, who probably hadn't been
inside a church during his adult lifetime, suddenly found a deep belief
in God and began attending services regularly after his wife died
unexpectedly of a heart attack. Instead of feeling cheated by God, he
felt welcomed, supported and loved by the same God that presumably
took our other friend's daughter so cruelly.

It is a kind of paradox that death (or other major loss) can cause
some people to turn toward God and others to turn away. Each of
these friends of ours suffered the same kind of loss, an early death,

suddenly, without closure, and impacting others in the family. What was it about them that made their outcomes so different?

While no one can say for certain how it will turn out, I think that any major loss that impacts us so deeply will cause most people to re-examine their belief systems in its wake. I certainly did. In *Loving Allie, Transforming the Journey of Loss*, I wrote about how I have moved through several religious systems to come to a place of not being religious at all, but rather being more spiritual, and hopefully a better person. Part of my own journey has taken me to a place of believing that my current lifetime on this earth is not the first time I've been here. I believe in past lives. To me they explain lots of things I've experienced in this one, like feelings of déjà vu, getting off a plane in Stockholm for the first time and yet recognizing the place and knowing deep inside that I had lived there before, or meeting someone and having an instant, deep knowing of that person as if we had been together before.

Now you may not believe in past lives, and I totally understand if you don't. I didn't either for about forty years of my life. Then a friend gave me a small book called, *Many Lives, Many Masters*, by Brian Weiss. Weiss is an M.D. psychiatrist who had a patient that went into spontaneous past life regression during his treatment of her. He, too, was a skeptic, at first. But working with her, and now, decades later, after having worked with hundreds or thousands of other patients like her he is not only a believer, but one of the best writers in the field. His latest book on past lives is called, *Miracles Happen*, and he co-authored it with his daughter.

After reading Weiss, I decided to try past life regression and I did it twice, both times with the same therapist. (Spoiler alert: I was never Cleopatra or anyone famous in a past life.) My therapist was wonderful. She hypnotized me and told me to just let my mind wander to wherever it needed to go and stop at anything that seemed important or significant to me. Here's what I recalled under hypnosis.

I experienced all of the following as a kind of flashback, I was fully present in the scene described below and it felt like it was happening in current time. I was there. It was real.

In one of my past lives I was a bush woman living in southern Africa. It was a hot, dry, desert setting. I was really old and small and had skin that was like leather. It was black skin but it had a kind of white powdery substance on it due to the dryness. My feet had hard callouses on the bottom from years of walking barefoot through the bush. I had family in my village and I may have been the oldest member of the community.

I knew that it was my time to die. I wasn't scared about that, maybe a little sad, but definitely not panicked. When I knew I was dying, I just left my community and walked out into the desert by myself. I didn't want to be a bother to them and I knew that my journey had to be a solo one as well. After walking for a time, I was tired and I lay down on the hot sands and curled up into a fetal position.

Then I simply let go. It was so easy and so peaceful.

Next, I could see my shriveled, wrinkled, old body curled into its little ball and I was rising above it. I had a realization that my body had died and that I still existed in a spiritual form, freed of the pain of old age and whatever actually caused my death. I also had the sensation of being much larger as a spiritual being than I had been as a bush woman.

That death was a natural, peaceful death. There was no struggling to hold on or stay here longer. It was just the most natural transition from the physical realm to the spiritual realm that could possibly happen.

When that session was over, I felt completely at peace. I also felt that the insights from the regression had been a blessing to me. I would call my death as a bush woman a good death. At the end of that regression I felt like I had been given the incredible gift of knowing how to die. It took away the fear of my own death.

In the second regression I was a Native American woman. (I actually have Cherokee heritage on both sides of my family, so this wasn't too much of a stretch.) My people lived on a mountainside in small dwellings that we had actually carved into the rocks. It was a kind of apartment community where other families had rock dwellings, too. There were lots of people in our community. We were very happy together. We had plenty of food and water. Everything was shared. No one considered that they "owned" anything. It was all community property and there was no such thing as poverty, or wealth for that matter. We worked hard. We had enough.

In that life I was artistically talented. I wove beautiful blankets and I painted designs on pottery that we made. It was very satisfying to me to be so creative, as I have no artistic talent in this life.

Because we lived on a mountain we could see way off in the distance for many, many miles. Usually those were beautiful sights to behold.

But, one day, as I was looking down into the valley off in the distance I saw horses coming. And riding those horses were many white men. They were European settlers who were coming into our area. This sight struck me with terror and great sadness. I knew in a flash that these invaders were coming to harm us and to take away our lands. It was truly a horrible realization. And I knew we were powerless to stop them.

I began sobbing deeply. What I saw in this regression was the death of our culture and our spirits. This was a tragic death. It was brutal. It was not natural. It was simply wrong. There was nothing good about it.

Now, you may say this was all a product of my vivid imagination, or that the therapist planted these ideas in my mind when she hypnotized me. I felt each of these experiences so profoundly that it doesn't matter to me how I had these memories, because I got two very important life lessons from them.

The first is how to die. The best way to die is to simply let go, to accept that every one of us is going to die and that dying is just as natural as being born. It may be painful and scary, but so is birth. And the more that we can simply surrender and release our fear of this great unknown the more likely we will have a good death.

When I was preparing for my labor with Geoff and Allie, the nurses taught me to concentrate on my breaths when the pain came. Focusing on my breathing took my fear away and allowed me to relax into the contractions rather than tense up and fight against them. What if we could use a kind of Lamaze breathing system for our deaths? Or, if we can't concentrate on our breaths, maybe we could have some beautiful music playing in the background that would be soothing to our souls? I think we have some work to do to create an atmosphere for the dying that is as nurturing and supportive as the new birthing environments are for those coming in the other door.

The second lesson I learned from my past life experiences is about the death of the spirit. There is nothing beautiful or natural about this kind of death. Our spirits are not supposed to die. They are the part of us that is eternal. But sometimes in life people do things to us that kill our spirit. They wound us. They leave us feeling broken in our most fragile parts. My lesson as a Native American woman was to avoid anything that makes me feel like it would kill my spirit. My spirit is something I am supposed to protect at all costs and it would be worth dying for. I react strongly now whenever I feel that I am back in that scary, spiritual death kind of place.

1. What do you believe happens to us when we die? Do you believe in either an after life or a past life? Write your beliefs in the space below. And, if you haven't made up your mind yet about your beliefs then write what steps you could take to help you decide.

    _____

    _____

    _____

    _____

    _____

    _____

    _____

    _____

Loss Doesn't Render Us Powerless

"New beginnings are often disguised as painful endings."

Lao Tzu

WHEN WE SUFFER a great loss part of our suffering is due to a feeling of helplessness. We replay the tape of what happened over and over again in our minds asking what did I do wrong; why didn't I see this coming; and why didn't I stop it from happening? This kind of self-abuse makes us feel powerless in the face of any major loss, especially the death of a loved one.

Statistically speaking, if you live long enough, people you love will die. You may not see it coming. You won't be able to prevent it. And you didn't cause it. Death happens. It happens to every one of us. And it will happen with increasing frequency as the Baby Boomer generation ages.

The National Funeral Directors Association reports that by 2030 3.3 million Americans will die each year. This is an increase of 32% from our current annual death rates. When we think of the families of those who will die, the numbers of Americans who will be dealing with loss issues comes closer to 10 million or more.

And, the rates of suicide are also increasing. From 1999-2010 the suicide rate among Americans aged 35-64 rose by nearly 30%. Far more middle-aged men commit suicide than women. The largest jump in suicide rates was among men in their fifties, where it increased by 50%. This is pretty sobering news, especially when we consider that suicide is vastly under reported. More Americans die of suicide than by car accidents, according to the Centers for Disease Control. In 2010 there were 33,687 car-related deaths, and 38,364 deaths by suicide.

The prevalence and inevitability of death requires us to talk about it and think about it in different ways lest we elevate death to some omnipotent force that renders us powerless in its wake.

What Can Be Done?

When my mother lay dying the hospice workers told our family that it was important for us to tell her that it was okay with us for her to go, to give her our permission and our blessing as she died. That seems like a little thing, but from their years of experience when the family is clinging to the dying and refusing to face reality it complicates the death process, making it harder for the person who is dying.

Often when someone dies in my family other family members in their presence describe seeing the spirits of our ancestors at the bedside. When my grandfather died, my mother said she saw his father in the room just before he died. She also said she saw angels surrounding his heart space. She ran out of the room to get my sister to come and see it, too, but when they reentered the spirits were gone. Just before my grandmother died she started talking to her husband, who was long deceased. When asked who was there, she said, "It's your grandfather. Can't you see him standing at the foot of the bed?"

You may think this is strange, or perhaps you, or your family, have similar stories.

If you have a belief system that includes a faith in God, or a belief in angels, then it isn't inconceivable that a dying person would be in the presence of holy beings as he or she was making the final transition, whether you could see them or not.

I recently received word that a wonderful woman, whom I had known for over forty years, was near death after a protracted battle with cancer. I was about 3,000 miles away from her when I heard the news. So I did what I could, which was to send her love and light.

In a quiet meditative state, in the wee, small hours of the morning I did this meditation for my friend, Marie.

Love and Light Meditation

Marie, I'm seeing you now on your deathbed and your body has taken a terrible pounding in the last few years. It's been prodded, poked, radiated, and infused with chemicals while it was also being attacked by cancer. You have fought the brave fight.

Now, as you lie there, barely aware of the world around you, I see your beautiful spirit. It is much larger than that shell which has contained it these past years. It is radiant, vibrant energy. It is pure joy and love.

And I see the spirits of others around you. These other spirits have long ago shed their physical shells. They are large, vibrant, beautiful beings that surround you with light and love. Perhaps you knew them in this life. Perhaps they were your family members. They know you at a deep soul level and you know them.

I see your spirit's divine energy merging with the divine energy of these other beings. I see you being drawn toward them and moving away from your physical being to become one with them.

You glance back at your withered body with grateful appreciation for how well it served you in this life and you simply let go. *You release it and you move beyond it.*

You, dear Marie, with whom we have laughed and loved, have made the transformation back to the source from which we came. Your life here is done.

Those of us who have loved you in this life send you love and light for your journey ahead.

That meditation gave me a lot of comfort as it felt that I was somehow helping Marie even though I was far away. By focusing my energy and my love on her so intensely, I felt that she was actually benefitting from my meditation practice. You may draw your own conclusions, of course.

The *Tibetan Book of Living and Dying* is filled with sage advice about practices the living can do for the dying and the dead. Tibetans are much more comfortable talking about death and preparing for it than we Westerners are. Of course the basis for their practice is Buddhism, but most of the meditations or exercises described in the book could simply be modified to fit other spiritual belief systems.

Death Meditation

If you find yourself at the bedside of someone who is dying and the death is imminent, the Tibetan practice is to sit quietly, breathe deeply and slowly, and hold the following imagery in your mind as they die.

Imagine that whatever being you believe is holy -- God, Jesus, Mary, Buddha, Allah, etc. -- is hovering in the air just above the person who is dying. See that the holy being is sending rays of pure golden light. Visualize rays of that light so bright that they fill the entire room. The light is directed at the dying person and surrounds his or her entire being. The light is comforting, healing, warm, and holy.

Now imagine that the dying person is aware of this divine presence and experiences the blessing of the light. See the dying person's own energy begin to coalesce and to rise up from his or her body. See that their energy is also pure golden light, light that is comforting, healing, warm, and holy.

And in your mind's eye see the merger of the dying person's light with the light of the holy being. See them rejoined as one, just as a single drop of water falls into the ocean and becomes part of something that is mighty.

Now, when you look at the empty shell which once encased the spirit of your loved one let your heart be filled with gratitude for the protection it provided, the warmth, the solace. Bless the body of the deceased as you release it. Its work is done.

Hold the thought of your loved one's blissful merger of spirit with spirit for as long as you can. Let your heart be filled with the loving kindness that the presence of the holy being brought to the dying. And know for certain that one day you too, will be making this transition back to source.

Take a slow, deep breath. Release it. Be at peace.

Some After Death Practices

In Judaism, there are special rites and rituals that follow the death of a loved one. The Hebrew word shiva means seven. In their belief system, whenever one of seven relatives, a father, mother, son, daughter, brother, sister, or spouse dies, then an observant Jew is required to sit for seven days in the home of the deceased in a state of mourning. The mourners stay at home all week and sit on low stools or on the floor to symbolically represent their feeling low or sad.

Each day of shiva three prayers services are conducted at the home, by men if the family is Orthodox, and by both men and women in non-Orthodox families. The Jewish prayer for the dead is called the Kaddish. When Allie died, her dear friend Melissa Schwab went to the morgue to say the Kaddish over her body. Although we aren't Jewish, I felt that her prayer was a blessing on Allie and on us all.

In the Jewish tradition mourners must not shave, take a full bath, wear leather shoes, wash their clothes, or have sexual relations during the seven-day period. Mourners also rip their shirt, vest or jacket before leaving the gravesite and continue to wear this garment for the full seven days to express their grief.

Tibetans believe that the first forty-nine days after someone's death mark the period that they are in the bardo, or intermediate state, of becoming, preparing to reincarnate into their next life. In the first twenty-one days the deceased's ties to this life are the strongest and they are most influenced by what their loved ones do in terms of ceremony or ritual. They also believe that the same day of the week that someone died is an important and powerful day on which to do work to help the dead in their journey either to the next life or to liberation.

Upon the death of a loved, one family members might do a phowa, which is a kind of meditation that envisions the Buddha light merging with the light of the deceased. This meditation might be done every day for the first twenty-one days and on the same day of the week for the first forty-nine days after the death. Additionally, any time they think of the deceased they chant the mantra: Om Mani Padme Hum (pronounced Om Mani Pémé Hung) to purify any negative emotions that might cause rebirth.

Not being a religious person, I don't follow any of these practices described above, but I can understand the need for them. When someone we love dies it feels as if the entire world has been badly shaken, like being in a major earthquake. Previously up was up and down was down, but now suddenly down is up and up is down. We feel lost, dazed, confused, angry, sad, guilty, and sometimes relieved, which can make us feel even guiltier.

So having a religious or spiritual ritual to fall back on can begin to restore order to our world. I'm sure that while sitting shiva many Jews come to accept their loss and begin to see that life continues beyond it, just as many Tibetans after fifty days must be more at peace with the state of their loved ones' journey to the next life or to liberation.

For a lot of Christians the ritual ends at the gravesite. When the dirt is sprinkled onto the casket, they leave and return to their homes to mourn, mostly without structure. The feeling of powerlessness is partly about not being sure what we are supposed to do now.

So it might be a good idea to invent some rituals that you could do for the dead if you don't already have them. Here are a few that I like.

1. When someone we love dies we keep a candle burning for thirty days. Because I believe that at death we are released from our physical state and our spirit is reunited with source, I light the candle to help guide a loved one's path back to the light of source. We have a LED candle going right now for our dear friend Katie. Each time I pass it, the delicate flicker reminds me of her and I send a little blessing to her spirit.

2. I do a Love and Light meditation just before someone I loves dies, even if I am not with them, when I am aware of their approaching death.

3. If I know someone is actually at their moment of death I do the meditation of their light merging with the God light as described above.

4. I look for signs of some sort of acknowledgement from the departed ones as a symbol that they are ok. When my parents died a pair of deer used to come into my yard and look directly into my eyes. I always felt it was my mom and dad saying hello. When Allie died I received many such messages and I described them when I wrote *Loving Allie, Transforming the Journey of Loss.*

    Rituals don't have to relate to the death itself. They can be any observance that helps bring you peace or a feeling of connection and closure. For example, you might plant a tree in memory of your loved one, donate to a charity, walk a labyrinth while thinking of them, or even name a star in their memory.

5. What are your death rituals? If a truthful answer is you don't have any, list some ideas you have for ways you could begin to honor and support someone's death journey.

    _____

    _____

    _____

    _____

The folks at the University of Washington are trying to get us to talk about death more openly with their Death Over Dinner project. The Department of Communication has created a website with free resources available online to facilitate conversations about how we want to die, what we feel about death, etc. The project started when they realized that although 75% of Americans say they want to die at home, only 25% actually do. Most die in hospitals or nursing facilities in environments that are not conducive to a peaceful transition. It was launched in 2013 and now over 1,000 such dinners have been hosted in private homes in 17 countries. You can check it out at, deathoverdinner.org.

Since the dinner table is one of the more forgiving places to have difficult conversations, they encourage us to host a gathering of family members or friends and share with each other what our final wishes are, whether we would want to be put on life support, would we want our organs donated, and more. Judging from their website, this kind of conversation, although difficult, is liberating and brings a sense of peace.

You may not host a dinner but you owe it to your family and friends to make your wishes known before it is too late. Perhaps the start of that kind of sharing can be with making up your mind first. Trust me on this advice. Even if you are not able or ready to answer the questions listed below, at least skim over them for now and promise yourself that you will complete this section when you are ready.

When someone dies families have to make decisions under the worst possible circumstances. Differences of opinion among family members can lead to family rifts that may never be healed. To the extent that each one of us takes the initiative to confront the types of questions listed below and make our wishes clearly known to our families we can leave them feeling more comforted when we are the ones who die.

6. When you die, do you want to be buried or cremated?

   _____

7. What do you want to have happen with your remains, will they be buried or scattered, or kept in some kind of container?

   _____

   _____

   _____

   _____

8. Do you want to be put on life support, if so, under what circumstances? If not, under what circumstances?

   _____

   _____

   _____

   _____

9. Would you want your organs or body parts to be donated to science or to others?

   _____

10. Have you made a will to dispose of your personal possessions after you die?

    _____

11. Have you made a living will to direct others what to do about your final medical issues?

    _____

12. Do you want to die at home, if that is possible?

_____

13. What type of memorial service would you want?

_____

_____

_____

_____

14. Do you have children who would need a guardian to take care of them in the event of your death? If so, whom would you appoint? Who would be the alternate if the person you name can't or won't serve?

_____

_____

_____

_____

15. Do you have pets whose care would need to be provided for when you die? If so, whom would you appoint as their caretaker?

_____

_____

_____

_____

Most of these issues can and should be addressed with an attorney as you plan for your will. But before seeking legal counsel you need to decide these kinds of issues for yourself so you can give guidance to your attorney. Some of your answers will need to be shared with your immediate family members so they will know what your wishes are. This is especially helpful when family members are faced with the decision of whether to resuscitate or put someone on life support.

I know that what I have just asked you to do is hard. But having done this myself, I can assure you that when you have addressed these end-of-life issues there is a feeling of closure and satisfaction that comes with its completion.

Instead of continuing as a culture of death deniers, by talking more openly about death-related issues before we are in a state of crisis, we could begin to shift the power and control away from death and claim it for ourselves. I don't know about you, but for me, being able to make these decisions about how my own life ends is important. It was important enough to decide my answers to all the questions I've asked you to consider and to make my wishes known to my family.

Before my mother died, she had a number of strokes, any one of which could have killed her. As she lay in intensive care we siblings rushed to her side, fearful of the outcome. But we didn't doubt one thing; our mother had told us many times that she never wanted to be kept alive on machines. She was very clear that a do not resuscitate order was what she wanted. So, even though we had lots of stress related to whether she would live or die, we were united as a family on the instructions to the medical team. That gave us a lot of peace in an otherwise terrible situation.

When you are ready or able to do so, my hope is that you will return to the questions above and answer them, and then share your answers with those whom you love.

What Am I Mad About, Sad About, Scared About?

"There is no greater illusion than fear."   Lao Tzu

A JOURNEY OF LOSS usually begins with an ending. Someone we loved died. A relationship or marriage ended. We ended a career path we had been on for a long time.

1. On the lines below make a list of at least twenty endings you have already faced in your life to date. They can be small or large matters. For example, graduation from high school is an ending.

    1.
    2.
    3.
    4.
    5.
    6.
    7.
    8.

9.

10.

11.

12.

13.

14.

15.

16.

17.

18.

19.

20.

An ending creates a space in our life. Just like pouring some wine out of a decanter makes a space for new wine to be added, an ending creates space in our life for something new to enter.

In *Loving Allie, Transforming the Journey of Loss,* I wrote about a special rites of passage ceremony that my Star Sisters and I created to mark Allie's entry into womanhood at the onset of her menarche. In that ceremony Allie (who was 12) and I were tied together at our waists with some sisal. We were each given a pair of scissors and had to make the decision to cut the symbolic umbilical cord that bound us.

In cutting it, Allie was signifying an end of her childhood and a willingness to enter womanhood as an independent person, no longer looking to me to mother her as I had when she was little. I had to decide to let go of her as my child and accept her as a young adult, my friend, and my equal. These decisions were all significant endings in our lives as mother/daughter. By ending the old paradigm we allowed a new relationship to develop between us that was healthy and fulfilling. I consider her rite of passage ritual one of the best things I ever did as a mother.

2. Look back over your list of endings. For as many as you possibly can, list any new thing that filled the space created by the ending.

1.
2.
3.
4.
5.
6.
7.
8.
9.
10.
11.
12.
13.
14.
15.
16.
17.
18.
19.
20.

As you review your list of endings, it may be that some of them feel like unfinished business. Yes, something ended and you filled the space that was created with something else, but there is still an emotional tug in your gut whenever you think about what happened. If that is the case, you have more work to do. You may be still carrying feelings of anger, sadness or fear associated with the loss.

What Am I Mad About?

We saw in the last chapter that even feelings of anger can help us move beyond a state of prolonged grief. So let's see if we can apply that insight to revisit any unfinished endings.

3. List below any of your endings that you still carry anger about. In addition to listing the ending, state what it is that makes you feel angry. For example, I am angry that when I got a divorce my ex got custody of the cat.

_____

_____

_____

_____

There are many ways to express our feelings of anger that can be healthy and helpful. I am not suggesting that you go back and confront someone about a wrong that happened in the past. Rather, I'm suggesting some behaviors in the present that can shift the way you feel about past wrongs.

It is not healthy to stuff anger. In fact, if you stuff your anger long enough you may become depressed, or develop stress-related illnesses. Freud first warned about the connection between anger turned inward and depression in his classic paper, *Mourning and Melancholia.*

In states of anger and depression there are similarly low levels of activity of the neurotransmitter serotonin. Depressed people can become quite aggressive.

So here are a couple of exercises that I have personally used to express my anger that don't threaten or harm anyone. Sometimes after doing them I actually feel silly or even tired. What I don't feel is angry any longer. Maybe they will work for you.

4. This one is simple. Go into a room by yourself and close the door. A bedroom is ideal for this exercise. Put a pillow over your face and scream as loudly as you can for as long as you can. Repeat as necessary.

I don't remember who taught me to do the scream pillow trick, but it works. The pillow muffles the sound of my screaming so no one else even has to know I'm upset. When I'm done, I feel relieved. And I often realize that I was wrong to be angry with the person or circumstance that provoked me. The screaming allows me to convert anger to a higher level of consciousness like acceptance or reason.

5. The next one requires some preparation, a witness, and the right location. You will need a plastic baseball bat, a pair of heavy-duty gloves (like the kind you would use for yard work), and a tree stump in a private place. The witness is important because you will be verbalizing your anger this time and having someone to hear your words validates them as true and real for you. Also the witness can encourage you to go further, or say more than you might do if you were alone. And the witness can keep you safe, if you might get too carried away by your anger.

    Basically, you will put on the gloves, pick up the plastic bat, and while beating it against the stump just yell out your angry thoughts at the top of your lungs. It's okay to use words like "I hate you," or scream expletives if you feel the need. No one is going to see or hear you except your witness. And if you've picked the right witness, absolutely no one is going to judge you or think you mad.

    We have used this exercise with many clients at the Maui Transitions Center. They start out thinking this is a weird thing to do. But with a little encouragement and the assurance that they will not be judged for it they really get into letting their anger rip. We have actually had people hit the stump so hard and so often they break the plastic bat. And before we started using the heavy-duty gloves some would rub blisters on their hands from the intensity of their anger work.

    A word of caution. Do not do this exercise anywhere near the vicinity of children. It would be hard to explain the need for this so that they would understand. And the last thing we would want is for our anger work to create fear in others.

What Am I Sad About?

6. Now review your list of endings again to see if there are any that continue to cause feelings of sadness for you. If there are, list the ending and describe what you think is causing your sadness.

    _____

    _____

    _____

    _____

Sadness is not the same thing as depression. The treatment of depression requires professional, medical care. If you think you are depressed, please reach out to a trusted therapist or Psychiatrist for assistance. Sadness is a temporary state. We all experience it at times and it usually passes fairly quickly. But if you are carrying around some sadness here are some top tips for ways to convert it to happiness.

- Hang around happy people.
- Keep a gratitude journal.
- Watch funny movies.
- Hug someone, especially a child.
- Go be outside in nature.
- Get some exercise.
- Do something good for someone else anonymously.
- Have a massage or soak in a bubble bath.
- Eat a healthy diet.
- Play with puppies or kittens.

7. When I feel a wave of sadness coming over me I sometimes throw myself a pity party. The purpose of a pity party is to indulge sadness, not run from it. For me, it means filling a bathtub with

bubble bath, playing some sad music, lighting some candles, and sitting in the stillness and forcing myself to think about the sadness. When the tears start to trickle I try to force them to become a flow and then a downpour. I moan, rock, and wail.

A pity party is exhausting work. And not long after it starts I'm usually sick of the indulgence, tired of the effort required to keep crying so much and also sitting in a bathtub of cold water. So I'm happy enough to blow out the candles, turn off the sad music get out of the tub, dry off and get on with my life.

If you decide to try this technique do it when no one else is around. A pity party is kind of a pathetic thing and really shouldn't be inflicted on others.

The reason it works is that when you force yourself to go deeper into your sad feelings you begin to realize that you are actually in charge of your feelings. Bad things happen to us, but we choose our response to them. You can choose to cry a little bit, a lot, or not at all. It isn't long before choosing to cry not at all feels like a really good option.

What Am I Scared About?

In his first inaugural address President Franklin D. Roosevelt famously said, "The only thing we have to fear is fear itself." Being scared or afraid can be a good thing if used in the proper quantities. We are right to be afraid of certain dangerous circumstances so that we don't subject ourselves to harm unnecessarily. But some fears are completely disproportionate to the actual risk involved.

Let me give you an example from my life. Several years ago, Will and I were on a holiday in Mexico in the Yucatan. We stayed at a beautiful resort that consisted of a series of casitas spread over about fifty acres of lush, tropical grounds. Each casita was completely private and somewhat isolated. There were no phones in the rooms, nor were there televisions. It was a chance to get away from it all and really relax.

But one night when I finished my shower, I opened the shower curtain to see a man's face staring at me through the window. It was terrifying. I screamed loudly and he ran off. When Will came into the bathroom I told him what happened. His immediate response was to run outside and try to catch the guy. When he couldn't, his second response was to report what happened to the management, which meant leaving me alone and feeling quite vulnerable fearing that the guy might double back to the casita. I was very afraid.

When the manager came I gave a description of the man, whose face I could never forget. And the next morning I picked him out of a line up before we left the property to return home.

I thought I had dealt with the crisis and it was part of the past. We flew home and put it behind us. But a couple of years later we went on a vacation in Hawai'i to another resort that was similar in design to the Mexican casitas, private cottages with thatched roofs, lush tropical plantings all around, warm, tropical air, etc. We were having a lovely time, enjoying the beach and pool activities.

But when I went to take a shower I had a flashback to the earlier incident. This time there was no peeping Tom. Standing in the shower I started crying and shaking again as if I were back in Mexico.

I was having an episode of post-traumatic stress. The amygdala region of my brain had decided that there were enough cues that were the same as the first incident to conclude that I was again at risk for danger. So it triggered a primitive kind of fight or flight response. I started crying and trembling again and we had to leave the hotel immediately.

I recently read that Jackie Kennedy also had post-traumatic stress after the assassination of President Kennedy in 1963. Unfortunately for her, the condition had not been diagnosed at that time. It was the return of traumatized Viet Nam war veterans that caused therapists to realize that their flashbacks needed new modalities of treatment.

My fear response was completely disproportionate to the risk the second time around. We call that an amygdala hijack, because the amygdala is the region of the brain that stores our fear memories and decides to take action. The knee-jerk reaction that my brain had was unwarranted by the current circumstances, just like the post-war responses of veterans, or Mrs. Kennedy's post-assassination traumas and fears.

When we returned home from the trip, I saw a therapist for treatment. She used Eye Movement Desensitization Reprocessing (EMDR) to reprocess my brain's reaction to the trauma. It was very effective therapy. In addition, she helped me develop a positive suggestion to use whenever I feel the fear again. It was to slay my own dragons. Now I don't expect someone else to rescue me or to fix the problem. Years later, if anything threatens me the thought "slay your own dragons!" pops into my mind and I just do what it takes to address the problem.

I have never had another episode of post-traumatic stress. It took only two sessions with the therapist and cost about $150.00, per session, money well spent. Will has also used EMDR therapy in moving through his journey of grief, again with a good outcome. If you want to read more about it, check out www.emdria.org for a list of certified EMDR therapists near you.

8. Look back over your list of endings and see if there are any that you are still scared about. Be specific about what you fear. Also, make notes if you think the fear is rational in your current circumstances, or irrational.

    _____

    _____

    _____

    _____

If you are having irrational fears about something that happened in the past you may want to consider seeking therapy to help you resolve it like I did.

Rational fear is a healthy defense mechanism. But you may want to control it even so. Here are some steps you can take to control your fears when they arise.

- Ascertain if you are actually at risk. Turn on the lights; look under the bed; look in the closet; check the locks on all the doors, etc.
- Don't subject yourself to fearful situations. If you are afraid of being out alone at night, avoid going out or ask a friend to accompany you when you must.
- Hold yourself in an assertive posture. This not only builds confidence and self-esteem, but also makes us seem larger and more formidable to others. Don't slouch around looking like an easy mark.
- Use slow, deep breaths to lower your heart rate and reduce your stress levels while you assess the level of actual risk.
- Take a self-defense class to prepare for handling a threatening situation should one arise.

And remember this; the ending that caused your fear is on the list because you have already lived through it. You have already survived it. It is part of your past.

I think the last word on fear should be from Eleanor Roosevelt who faced many fears in her personal life. She said: "You gain strength, courage and confidence by every experience in which you really stop to look fear in the face. You are able to say to yourself, I have lived through this horror. I can take the next thing that comes along. You must do the thing you think you cannot do."

Whom Do I Need to Forgive?

"In the end, the treasure of life is missed by those who hold on and gained by those who let go."   Lao Tzu

FORGIVENESS IS A cornerstone of every religion.

Christians who recite the Lord's Prayer ask to be forgiven for their trespasses as they forgive others who trespass against them. The last words spoken by Christ were a plea to God to forgive the ones who killed him, for they "know not what they do." And in Matthew, the teaching was to be ready to forgive over and over again. "Then Peter came to Jesus and asked, 'Lord, how many times shall I forgive my brother when he sins against me? Up to seven times?' Jesus answered, 'I tell you, not seven times, but seventy-seven times.'" Matthew 18: 21-22.

Buddhists believe that hatred leaves a lasting negative effect on our karma and forgiveness has a wholesome effect. Buddha said, "You will not be punished for your anger. You will be punished by your anger. Holding onto anger is like grasping a hot coal with the intent of throwing it at someone else but you are the one who gets burned."

In Sikhism, forgiveness is viewed as the remedy to anger. "Where there is forgiveness there is God himself." Adi Granth, Shalok, Kabir, p. 1372

And Taoism teaches us to, "Show endurance in humiliation and bear no grudge." *Treatise on Response and Retribution.*

Judaism teaches its practitioners to ask for forgiveness when they have wronged another and sets aside the holiday of Yom Kippur as a day of atonement when Jews stop harmful behaviors, express regret for them, and repent. In the Jewish teachings a wronged person is religiously required to forgive anyone who sincerely apologizes. According to the Torah, it is forbidden to be obdurate and not allow yourself to be appeased when asked by an offender for forgiveness. "Who takes vengeance or bears a grudge acts like one who, having cut one hand while handling a knife, avenges himself by stabbing the other hand." *Talmud*, Nedarim 9.4

And in Islam, forgiveness is a prerequisite for genuine peace. Although the Qur'an makes some exceptions for violence in defense of faith, property, or life, it still teaches that forgiveness is the better course of action whenever possible. "O you who believe! Among your spouses and children there may be enemies for you, so beware of them. Yet, if you pardon, forbear, and forgive (their faults towards you and in worldly matters), then (know that) God is All-Forgiving, All-Compassionate." *Qur'an* 64.14

Maybe, like me, you aren't a religious person and these scriptures have no power of persuasion for you on the importance of forgiveness. Perhaps science would be more persuasive.

The Harvard Medical school has spent more than fifty years studying how life choices make the difference in those who age well and lead happier, healthier lives well into their seventies, eighties and beyond. One of their surprising findings was that "Healing relationships are facilitated by a capacity for gratitude, for forgiveness, and for taking people inside. (By this metaphor I mean becoming eternally enriched by loving a particular person.)" The book, *Aging Well, Surprising Guideposts to a Happier Life,* by George E. Vaillant, M.D., has become such a great teacher for Will and me that we regularly give it to friends and family.

And our friend Dr. David R. Hawkins, whom I wrote about in Chapter 3, showed us that while grief has a level of consciousness of only 75, forgiveness, and acceptance take us to a level of 350, which is exponentially greater. It is only by rising to a level of forgiveness that we can hope to restore ourselves to a capacity for having love and joy in our lives again.

Finally, if neither religion nor science can convince you to forgive those who have wronged you, maybe you will do it for selfish reasons. You see, as long as we hold anger in our hearts against someone, they have power over us. It is only when we truly forgive, release and bless them that we are finally free of them.

I am not suggesting that you go find the person and tell them you forgive them. This is not a good idea. For me, forgiveness is an entirely private matter. It doesn't require the other person's involvement at all. They don't have to apologize or to even realize they have wronged us. If we wait around for an apology from them we may allow the wound to remain open forever. Forgiveness merely requires that you truly let go of the wrong and move on.

Which brings us to the question, whom do I need to forgive?

1. Think about the particular circumstances that cause you to be experiencing great loss in your life. Is there a person or persons whom you hold accountable or blame for what happened to you? If it is a career setback, perhaps you are angry with a work colleague. If you are grieving the loss of a marriage, perhaps you are still angry with your former spouse. If you are grieving the loss of a loved one, perhaps you are angry with someone or even your loved one for something that contributed to their death. On the lines below list every person or group that you need to forgive and briefly state what the offense was.

    _____

    _____

    _____

    _____

_____

_____

_____

_____

_____

Did you forget anyone? Think carefully about your list -- is there anyone else whom you didn't put on it? How about yourself? Are you punishing yourself for something that you did or failed to do that may have somehow made matters worse? For example, if you are grieving the loss of a marriage, do you feel at fault for certain aspects of it? If it is the death of a loved one, do you hold yourself responsible in some way?

2. On the lines below write anything you did or failed to do with respect to your loss issue that you may also be grieving.

_____

_____

_____

_____

A Forgiveness Meditation

3. Do this exercise when you are in a quiet place, without any distractions. Sit comfortably in a chair or perhaps on a pillow in the lotus position. Relax into a comfortable position and use the prompts below to take you through guided imagery. Just allow your mind to wander wherever the suggestion takes you. Don't evaluate. Just go with the imagery and trust the process.

With a little imagination, you can do this exercise by yourself. I'm going to give you the suggested prompts and after you read each one, just close your eyes and meditate on the words for a few minutes before going on to the next prompt. If you will slow down with this step and be open to where your imagination may take you, you may have some surprising insights.

To begin, inhale slowly through your nose to a count of one, two, three, four. Then hold your breath to the same count of four. Then exhale slowly through your mouth to the same count of four.

Now do it again, even slower this time.

And do it yet again.

Remember when we consciously slow down our breathing we are doing several things simultaneously. We are becoming mindful. We are reducing our stress levels. We are lowering our heart rate. We are signaling to our self that this is not just another unconscious breath among many millions we may take in a lifetime. This is different.

So when you have done at least three of these conscious breaths and are feeling more relaxed, slowly read through each of these guided imagery prompts and stay with whatever comes up for you through several more slow, deep breaths before you go on to the next prompt.

Now imagine that there is a stage in front of you. You are seated in the front row of the audience facing the stage. The theater is quiet and dark, except for the lights on the stage.

Now imagine that on the left side of the stage stands every person or every group that you listed in the forgiveness exercise above. It doesn't matter if there is only one or if there are many.

Just visualize everyone you need to forgive standing there waiting patiently for your cue.

And as you take another slow, conscious breath and slowly release it, imagine that the first one of them advances to the center of the stage. When they reach center stage, say aloud any words of forgiveness you need to express in order to feel completion with them. For example, "I forgive you for dying and leaving me all alone with these huge medical bills." Or, "I forgive you for drinking that night and speeding and losing control of the car." Use words that feel right to you.

With several more slow deep breaths, hold them at center stage until you feel yourself really releasing the inner knot of anguish you have been carrying along with the anger.

After you feel more relaxed about this particular person, imagine them walking slowly to the right of the stage.

Then, take another slow deep breath before you imagine the second person or group advance to center stage and repeat the process.

Do this visualization for every single person on the left side of the stage until you have advanced them to the right side of the stage.

When they are all on the right side, take another deep, slow breath and say these words aloud.

I forgive you all.

I release you all.

I bless you all.

If you need to forgive yourself for something you did or failed to do, imagine that you too are center stage and say aloud the words that you need to hear to feel closure. It might be "I forgive myself for not telling you I loved you," or I forgive myself for not listening to you more." Just use your own words in a way that feel authentic to you.

Slow down here, especially if you are forgiving yourself, and let it sink in that you too are capable of being forgiven and that you deserve to be released from any guilt you may have been carrying.

Take several slow, deep breaths until you feel a sense of satisfaction and closure.

And now imagine you are walking up the aisle, out of the theater. You are leaving on the stage all the emotional baggage you have been carrying around with you from these old wounds. Feel yourself becoming lighter with a spring in your step as you are freed of the weight that held you down.

And when you imagine yourself closing the theater door, see that as a symbol that the book is closed on all these wrongs. It is over. Done.

What Are My Resources?

"If you correct you mind, the rest of your life will fall into place."
Lao Tzu

ALTHOUGH YOU MAY not realize it yet, the single greatest resource available to help you recover from the setback of a major loss is you. No one else knows your suffering as deeply as you do. No one else will feel your shifts in consciousness, or the subtle insights you develop along the way, or the delicate changes that begin to signal progress is being made. Sure there are others who can help you, but the one who will ultimately make the difference in your journey back to a fulfilling life is you.

You need to be able to count on yourself to be reliable, to do the work that will be required, to get out of bed, to put one foot in front of the other and move on, to ask for help when you need it, to face the pain and work through it, and to love yourself enough to go on even when the going is really hard.

On the lines below I want you to make an honest inventory. Most of us don't give ourselves enough credit for our strengths. This is not the time for false modesty.

96

What Are My Strengths?

1. On the lines below make an inventory of your strengths. They can be skills, talents, or character attributes. Please list at least twenty strengths. If you need more space, then list two or more per line.

    1.
    2.
    3.
    4.
    5.
    6.
    7.
    8.
    9.
    10.
    11.
    12.
    13.
    14.
    15.
    16.
    17.
    18.
    19.
    20.

Look back over your list. Slowly take in the fabulous gifts you bring to any situation. You are a pretty amazing person! You have just made an inventory of many attributes you already possess that you can draw upon to help unslump yourself.

For some reason when we ask clients to make a similar inventory of their weaknesses, they have an easier time being hard on themselves than with the strengths inventory. But knowing our challenge areas and being realistic about where we may fall short can provide valuable insight, especially in highly stressful situations.

What Are My Weaknesses?

2. On the lines below make an honest inventory of your weaknesses or shortcomings. These may be habits, character attributes, personality traits, etc.

1.
2.
3.
4.
5.
6.
7.
8.
9.
10.
11.
12.
13.
14.
15.
16.
17.
18.
19.
20.

We don't ask you to list your weaknesses in order to bring you down. We want you to know these potential pitfalls so that you will avoid them. If you know there is a big hole in the road ahead, you detour around it. So if you are making good progress on your recovery from loss and then in a month from now you suddenly fall into a hole, you can look back at this inventory to help you understand where you went wrong. And by revisiting your strengths inventory you can pick from the menu of your strengths the precise ones that will help pull you back out of the hole.

Here's how it worked for me. One of my weaknesses is that under great stress I eat ice cream as a comfort food. It is bad for me and my forty-pound weight gain over the past three years is visible proof of just how bad it is. But one of my strengths is my intuition, my ability to see the big picture. And the big picture on indulging in ice cream is that it can give me diabetes or other major medical problems. Plus, after I've eaten it the problems don't go away. I've just added a new problem to my list of challenges.

From this review of my strengths and weaknesses, I was able to choose to use exercise as a means to reduce my stress levels. Will and I go for hikes in the beautiful Rocky Mountain National Park that is near our home. Exercise provides endorphins that lift our spirits. When my spirits are higher I don't need comfort food. Plus the exercise burns calories and results in weight loss.

As you look back over your inventories of your strengths and weaknesses pick one or two weaknesses that you can focus on as test cases to apply this technique. See for yourself if you can't also use your strengths to counteract your weaknesses.

When life serves us a season of difficulty it is easy to focus on our losses and our woes. We can fall into a habit of spending too much time thinking about what's wrong in our life and not enough about what's right. This is especially true when we are in crisis grief and the wound is new and perhaps we are still bleeding.

With the pity party exercise in Chapter 9, we tried to show you that you are in charge of your emotions. You can choose whether to wallow in your sadness or take steps to move beyond it, including therapy if you need it.

What is Right in My Life?

3. In the next exercise we want you to make an inventory of what is right in your life. What is it that you are grateful for? What are your blessings? List at least twenty of your blessings below. If you need more space, list two or more per line.

1.

2.

3.

4.

5.

6.

7.

8.

9.

10.

11.

12.

13.

14.

15.

16.

17.

18.

19.

20.

If you want to have better balance as you work to overcome the loss that you have suffered then keeping an ongoing inventory of your blessings can help give you the perspective that is needed. You could simply keep paper and a pen (or an iPad) by your bedside and before you go to sleep each night list five things you are grateful for that day. Imagine if you did this for a year. You would have a list of over fifteen hundred blessings in your life. That is powerful stuff.

Previously, in Chapter 1, we had you list the persons in your life who would be supportive of you on the journey of loss. And, in this chapter we have acknowledged that you are your single greatest resource and supporter. But there are additional helpers that we haven't discussed yet.

This next bit may sound strange to some of you, I admit. But hear me out. Many years ago, when I was working to resolve some of my early childhood issues, one of the therapeutic modalities was a birth regression. Sometimes, due to complications in the womb or traumatic birth experiences, we may form precognitive opinions about the world, based on whether our first contact with it was easy or difficult. This early experience may skew our perception about whether the world is a safe place or not and can impact our judgment and relationships many years, or even decades later.

There is an entire sub-specialty in therapy called pre and perinatal psychology that addresses these early childhood issues. It looks at how breech babies tend to approach things backwardly, or how incubated babies react to bright lights from above, or how preemies may lack warmth and ease of human contact due to being hospitalized for long periods after birth.

At a time in my life when I was making some pretty important decisions, I decided to work on my own early childhood traumas to attempt to be at peace with my past. And so I did a birth regression. The purpose of the regression is to have an adult, under hypnosis, remember exactly what happened to him or her in the womb. Then, working with a trained therapist, the individual re-experiences the birth in a positive and healthy environment in order to correct any bad effects from the first time around. So an adult who was born as a breech baby, for example, might be helped to turn into the correct position through a birth regression, or a Caesarian born adult might get to actually complete the birth process through a simulation.

In my case the therapist placed me under hypnosis and asked me to go back to my earliest recollections or impressions of this world. I did remember being very small and being in my mother's womb. But what else I remembered blew my mind, and my therapist's as well.

I remembered during my womb state that there were many other beings around me. They did not have bodies. They were large beings with no physical shape at all. I experienced them as good, protective, helpful beings, who had my best interests at heart. You may think of them like guardian angels, or saints, or a soul group, or any kind of divine beings that watch over someone. I didn't see them that way, just vibrational beings without shape, who loved me somehow.

During my womb experience I could communicate with these beings telepathically. No words were used at all, but they were sending me messages continuously and I was responding in kind. It was a blissful state. I felt safe, secure, loved, surrounded, and supported.

The therapist was getting a little worried because she was trying to give me suggestions to move my birth process along. She wanted me to go into the birth canal and be ready to be born. But I felt so wonderful just where I was that I wanted to stay there forever. It took her a very long time and many suggestions to get me to move past the re-experiencing of this memory.

As I described in *Loving Allie, Transforming the Journey of Loss,* my actual birth was uneventful. Being the eighth of ten children, my mother had this birth thing under control. There were no complications and I came into the world easily, from a medical perspective.

What happened, from a spiritual perspective, is that during my entire womb experience, my soul group, if you will, was right by my side, nurturing me, helping me and loving me. But at the moment I drew my first breath I lost contact with them. I could no longer feel their presence, or connect with them telepathically. It was like my taking on the density of a human body somehow blocked their communication with me. This disconnection was the trauma of my birth. It left me feeling so alone in the world. I may have been born into a large family where there was virtually no time or space to be alone, but a good part of my life has been spent feeling lonely and cut-off from my source.

With no small amount of effort, I have learned that if I am still and quiet, if I can clear my mind, slow my breathing and enter a meditative state, they are able to get through to me yet. And when that happens it feels like I'm in the groove. Life seems easier. I'm clearer about what path I'm supposed to take. I'm connected again to divine love and divine support.

4. As you think about your own journey, what spiritual resources are available to lift you up? How do you access divine guidance when you need it?

_____

_____

_____

_____

And now I want to share a tool with you. One of our clients in the Maui Transitions Center called it the most important tool she'd learned to help her manage life's changes. I wrote about this tool initially in *Loving Allie, Transforming the Journey of Loss*, but it bears repeating and further explanation.

Here's how it works. Our brains are composed of basically two hemispheres. The left brain, which can be accessed through the right hand, is primarily the portion where our rational thought occurs. The left brain is essential in helping us make wise decisions, understand the logic of things, solve problems and speak. The right brain, which can be accessed through the left hand, is mostly the creative side. It is where our best expressions of art, music, inspiration and intuition occur. These two halves are connected in the middle by the corpus callosum. But the beauty of how our brains work is that both sides work together, not in isolation. It is when we have the best of both logic and creativity that we make the best decisions or express our most creative genius.

The majority of people are right handed, and the majority of time is spent in the left-brain world. That usually serves us very well. However, when life deals us a major blow, like a divorce, or loss of job, or the death of someone we love we need more help than either half of our brain provides. We need 100% of our capacity for thinking, analyzing, inventing, creating, and growing and changing to help us recover. Grief can reduce our functioning capacity to less than optimal levels. We may miss some of the opportunities to help unslump ourselves without the use of a tool like the one described below.

We have used it for years at the Maui Transitions Center and have witnessed clients making major breakthroughs from its insights. I hope it will be helpful to you as well.

5. In this exercise you will be using your left and right brain functions, and both your left and right hands. The right hand is the dominant hand for about 90% of the world. If this is true for you, you will begin writing with your right hand. If, however, you are among the 10% for whom the left hand is dominant, you will begin writing with your left hand.

Beginning with your dominant hand, write a letter to whomever or whatever you have lost. See them or it clearly in your mind's eye as you begin. In the letter tell them whatever you need to say in order to get everything off your chest, to clear the air. For example, if they died without goodbyes, this is the time to say them. If you are angry about some aspect of the death experience, tell them in your letter. Similarly, if it was a divorce situation, write to your ex-spouse about everything you suffered as a consequence of the failed relationship. If you are grieving the loss of a career you may want to write the letter to your ex-boss or former partners. If you have unanswered questions, ask them.

Don't rush this part of the exercise. Slow down enough to get it all on the paper. Then take a break. Walk away from the exercise and get some fresh air.

The second part of the exercise begins by changing hands. Move your pen or pencil to your non-dominant hand and now write a letter to yourself *from* the dearly departed, or the ex-spouse, or former employer. Let your mind wander to wherever it needs to go. Don't inhibit your thoughts. Writing with your non-dominant hand, respond to all the questions or concerns that were raised in the original letter. Write until you feel you have truly dealt with everything and if something new pops into your mind, write about that, too.

For the last part of this exercise it helps to have a partner. Pick someone you trust, who has been supportive of you on your journey. If you want the maximum benefit from the exercise the person you pick should be the same gender as the person you wrote to in your letter.

Now you will read your first letter aloud to your partner. Read it slowly and allow your words to sink in as you say them. Then, ask your partner to slowly read aloud your response. When you hear the words written by your non-dominant hand, it seems as if they are actually coming to you directly from the deceased or the ex. I have found this to be the case, particularly when your partner is the same gender as the loved one you are grieving.

Having witnessed these letters being written, and answered for more than twenty years, I can assure you that this exercise can have a powerful impact on your healing process. Try it, and let me know how it works for you.

6. As a variation on the left-hand, right-hand exercise above, some clients have adopted a practice of using this approach to ask themselves questions whenever they feel stuck. It works effectively for self-inquiry as well. If, for example, you are making good progress in your journey but you still can't get past one issue, try having a left-hand, right-hand discussion with yourself. Just be

sure to ask the question with your dominant hand and answer with your non-dominant hand. If I'm really bothered by some irritation I start by asking myself, *"What's the lesson here?"* And then I let my creative side of my brain help me figure out what's really going on for me.

Finally, I want to suggest one more resource to help yourself transform your loss. It is so simple it could be done anywhere. We call it the cocktail napkin because you could literally do it on a cocktail napkin in a bar if you had to.

7. Think about your current situation, whether it is a loss due to a divorce, career change, death, or other major change. Then ask yourself four simple questions three times each: What do I think? What do I want? What do I need? What do I do? Going through three rounds of these questions takes you deeper and deeper with each iteration.

To show you how it works, let's return to my eating ice cream situation. Knowing it was bad for me, I still kept doing it for a couple of years. Here's how the exercise would work in my case.

Round One:
- What do I think? I think I'm eating too much Rum Raisin ice cream.
- What do I want? I want to stop it, and to eat healthier foods.
- What do I need? I need to have more willpower and to stop buying the ice cream.
- What do I do? I keep buying it every time we run out.

Round Two:
- What do I think? I think if I keep buying the ice cream, I'll just keep eating it.
- What do I want? I want to lose the weight!
- What do I need? I need to ask Will to remind me not to buy ice cream and to encourage me to lose weight.
- What do I do? I eat it and then I feel ashamed of myself.

Round Three:

- What do I think? I think I'm not listening to my own inner wisdom.
- What do I want? I want to be healthier and happier.
- What do I need? I need to figure out what the hole is in me that I'm trying to fill up with ice cream.
- What do I do? I start working on the underlying issue.

And that is how I broke the habit. I realized that I had more work to do on anger issues. It was because I was stuffing my anger and not resolving it that I was also stuffing my face. When I addressed the underlying issue, my need for obsessively eating ice cream went away. Now, Will and I are both on diets and are working out more and taking better care of ourselves.

On the lines below ask yourself for advice on any issue that is currently bothering you and see where your self-inquiry takes you.

Round One:

1. What do I think?

_____

_____

_____

_____

2. What do I want?

_____

_____

_____

_____

3. What do I need?

_____

_____

_____

_____

4. What do I do?

_____

_____

_____

_____

Round Two:

1. What do I think?

_____

_____

_____

_____

2. What do I want?

_____

_____

_____

_____

3. What do I need?

_____

_____

_____

_____

4. What do I do?

_____

_____

_____

_____

Round Three:

1. What do I think?

_____

_____

_____

_____

2. What do I want?

_____

_____

_____

_____

3. What do I need?

_____

_____

_____

_____

4. What do I do?

_____

_____

_____

_____

If you work through three iterations of this self-inquiry it will become quite clear to you what you need to do. But as the ancient Chinese philosopher Wang Yangming said, *"To know and not to do is not to know."*

Some Success Stories

"If you realize that all things change, there is nothing you will try to hold on to. If you are not afraid of dying, there is nothing you cannot achieve." Lao Tzu, *Tao Te Ching*

D R. ELISABETH KÜBLER-ROSS, the author of *On Death and Dying,* wrote, "The most beautiful people we have known are those who have known defeat, known suffering, known struggle, known loss, and have found their way out of the depths. These persons have an appreciation, sensitivity, and an understanding of life that fills them with compassion, gentleness, and a deep loving concern. Beautiful people do not just happen."

If you are stuck in the throes of grief it can be helpful to hear of others who have suffered the same, or even more than you, and who have managed to transcend their loss and come out of it a stronger, better person; a beautiful person. Here are a few success stories that may lift your spirits.

Before Theodore Roosevelt was the 26th President of the United States, before he was the head of the Republican Party, before he was the Governor of New York, and before he led the Rough Riders into Cuba, he was a sickly, asthmatic young man who was home schooled due to his physical weaknesses. His mother doted on him, and he adored his father. He fell in love at first sight and married a beautiful 19 year-old young woman, Alice Lee, who bore him a daughter three years later, also named Alice. On one day in February 1884, two days after baby Alice was born, both his mother and his wife died in the same house, his mother of typhoid fever and his beloved wife of Bright's disease. He was twenty-six years old.

Roosevelt was so heartbroken and in such a state of despair, he handed his newborn daughter over to his sister and fled from New York to the Badlands of North Dakota. He bought a ranch, learned to ride, rope, and drive cattle. He toughened up his body with strenuous exercise. He refused to give in to the asthma. He kept busy, very busy. He earned the respect of local cowboys for his efforts. And, when the worst winter on record froze most of his cattle to death, he returned to New York to become Governor, then Vice President, then the youngest President at age 42, he went on to build the Panama Canal, and to win a Nobel Peace Prize for negotiating and end to the Russo-Japanese war. He is consistently ranked as one of the greatest U.S. Presidents. And his likeness was carved into Mount Rushmore.

Before Oprah Winfrey became a billionaire media mogul, before she delivered nearly one million votes to presidential candidate Barack Obama, before she was a top-rated television host, film star, or publisher, she was a poor little girl from rural Mississippi, whose mother was an unwed teenager. Oprah was sexually abused from age 9, and at age 14 she gave birth to a son who died in infancy. Oprah openly discussed these terrible things that happened to her as the subject of one of her Life Classes on her television network, OWN TV. (You can watch her class at Oprah.com, "Oprah's Teen Pregnancy Leads to a Second Chance," a segment on Oprah's Life Class.)

She was sent to live with her father in Nashville. Because he prized education she was encouraged to get good grades in school. She became an honors student, was voted Most Popular Girl, and became active in oratory competitions. Her oratorical skills won her a college scholarship and ultimately a job with a local radio station that she held for several years. She was both the youngest news anchor and the first black female news anchor at Nashville's WLAC-TV.

At age 29 she moved to Chicago to host a local television talk show and when she succeeded in lifting its status to become the highest rated talk show in Chicago, she went on to national syndication and global fame.

Consider too, the case of Eleanor Roosevelt, who was both a niece and wife of U.S. Presidents. Her childhood was no bed of roses, in spite of great family wealth and fame. By the time she was eleven, both of her parents as well as her brother were dead. The biographer, Joseph P. Lash, described her as an insecure ugly duckling. Her marriage, at age 20, wasn't a happy one. It brought with it a controlling mother-in-law, and a husband who cheated on her with his secretary for the rest of his life, even after he developed polio.

Eleanor was the longest-serving First Lady of the United States. She campaigned and made public appearances on her husband's behalf when his disease made travel impossible. She held press conferences and wrote a syndicated newspaper column, and spoke at the Democratic National Convention, unprecedented behaviors for a First Lady. She was outspoken on racial issues, civil rights, and expanded roles for women in the workplace. She advocated for the U.S. to join the United Nations and became one of its first delegates. She was the first chair of the U.N. Commission on Human Rights and oversaw the drafting of the Universal Declaration of Human Rights. She was easily one of the most widely admired people of the 20th Century.

And one more example, this one from the sports arena, is the life of basketball great Larry Bird. Larry was the fourth-born into a poor family of six children in Indiana. His mother worked two jobs to support them. When he was in high school his parents divorced and the next year his father killed himself with a gun just after speaking on the phone with the family. (See *Drive, the Story of My Life*, by Larry Bird, and *Larry Bird*, by Mark Beyer.)

Larry used basketball to help cope with his pain and anger from his difficult home life. He practiced incessantly. When he grew four inches in his senior year of high school he used his new height to his advantage and received a college scholarship based on his talent. He played first for the Indiana Hoosiers and then for Indiana State, culminating in a championship playoff with Michigan State where he and Magic Johnson began their famous on-court rivalry. As a professional he played his entire career for the Boston Celtics, winning three NBA Championships and two NBA Finals Most Valuable Player Awards. In 1992 he was a member of the U.S. Dream Team that won the gold medal in the Summer Olympics. He served as coach and President of Basketball Operations for the Indiana Pacers after retiring from playing the game. He is the only man in NBA history to be named Most Valuable Player, Coach of the Year, and Executive of the Year. When we think of Larry Bird, it is of the champion he became and not of the losses he overcame before he was famous.

Larry Bird, Eleanor Roosevelt, Oprah Winfrey and Teddy Roosevelt became beautiful people precisely because they first knew defeat, suffering, struggle and loss and found their way out of the depths.

Envisioning Your Own Transformation

1. With these inspiring role models to guide you, think about what people may say about you in years to come, how you took the tragedy that befell you and turned it into some deeply meaningful work or purpose for the rest of your life. Spend some time quietly imagining the stories that will be told about the challenges you faced and how you overcame them. After you have been still and quiet with your thoughts, write below how you would like to transform the loss you have suffered into a positive experience.

    _____

    _____

    _____

    _____

"Whatever you can do, or dream you can do, begin it. Boldness has genius, power, and magic in it!" (Attributed to Goethe)

2. And now, be honest with yourself again. What changes would you need to make to see the transformation you envisaged become a new reality for you?

_____

_____

_____

_____

In Greek mythology, the phoenix, a colorful bird about the size of an eagle, is said to be reborn by rising from the ashes of a previous existence. It is precisely the descent and the destruction that it brings that makes the second rising so meaningful. The initial challenge for anyone who is trying to transform a journey of loss into a better reality is to believe that they too, can rise again.

I grew up hearing the axiom: "Seeing is believing," which is basically a requirement that the proof precede the belief. But I have come to learn that the opposite is not only truer but also more powerful. "Believing is seeing," is what the Baptists call stepping out on faith. If you believe something is true then you will find evidence to support your belief.

Here's how it works. Years ago Volkswagen reintroduced the classic Beatle, a modern interpretation of a car I had once driven in college. Mine was bright orange and had about 200,000 miles on it and a hole in the floor. The new one was coming out just as Allie was turning 16 and we decided to buy one for her, sight unseen. It was to be the first new Beatle on Maui. And the moment we made the decision suddenly new Beatles began appearing everywhere we went. It was as if we had put out a vibration in the universe that said we believe again in this car and the universe promptly began delivering evidence to us of our belief.

If you believe that you can transform the loss you have experienced into something that is positive and empowering in your life, then you will also begin to see the proof that you can do it. Your level of consciousness will rise to vibrations of hopefulness and optimism, and you will attract other hopeful and optimistic people who will match your vibration and help give you what you want.

Believing in your own personal power of transformation is the first step. If you believe, you will see the proof of your beliefs almost everywhere you go. And if you hold that belief long enough, you too, will rise from the ashes, like the phoenix.

3. Hold the meditation of your own personal transformation as you transform the black and white phoenix on the following page into something truly dazzling, filled with color and life.

    Be like the phoenix

©insima/Shutterstock.com

Legend has it that in the late Fifteenth Century a Japanese shogun, Ashikaga Yoshimasa sent a damaged Chinese tea bowl back to China to be repaired. The repairs were done with ugly metal staples. The belief is that this prompted Japanese craftsmen to devise a better, more aesthetic means of restoring precious damaged pottery and lacquer ware. Thus was born, Kintsugi, the Japanese art of fixing broken pottery with a resin mixed with gold, silver or platinum.

Tied to the practice was a philosophy that breakage and repair of an object are not things to be covered up or disguised, rather they are part of the object's history and add to its beauty and depth of meaning. The Japanese embraced the flawed and broken aspects of pottery in the same way that they accepted change and fate as merely aspects of the human experience, to which we are all susceptible.

As you continue your journey of transformation of loss, may you embrace the brokenness of your own spirit as well as the scars that show you have healed, and may you come to see that your beauty as a loving spirit has only deepened because of the brokenness you have endured. Like the golden repairs of Japanese pottery may you come to celebrate and honor the times when you were shattered by loss and to know that you too radiate a light that can help heal others. Not only are you stronger in your broken places, but you are more beautiful as well.

Honor the journey.

One More Thing

"When I let go of what I am, I become what I might be."

Lao Tzu

I F YOU HAVE made it to this point in the workbook you deserve a lot of credit. I have asked you to face some pretty tough issues and to be brutally honest with yourself throughout. You may well have shed a few tears along the way, but hopefully with those tears came some new insights about how you could transform the journey of loss that you have been on to a more positive outcome. You may have gotten angry, even with me, and you may have forgiven some people you previously blamed, including yourself.

If I have said anything herein that offended you, please accept my sincere apology. And please forgive me. I only intended to be of service to you.

The last exercise is an optional one for you to consider. I think you should do it and if you do I believe it will be something you will actually enjoy. It's a kind of pat on the back for a job well done.

1. In this exercise your assignment is to write a letter to yourself, giving yourself credit for all the effort you put into reading this book and doing the work assigned. Write any special insights you

received and any "Aha!" moments you experienced. Be sure to include any advice to yourself about things you must follow up on, or begin, or continue to do. This is no time for modesty. Sing your praises!

After writing your letter, put it in an envelope, address it to yourself and put the proper postage on it. Then place your self-addressed envelope inside a larger envelope and address that envelope to me:

Dayle E. Spencer
P.O. Box 4114
Estes Park, Co 80517

Be sure to add postage to both your letter to self and your letter to me before sending them.

When I receive your letter I will hold it for three months and then I'll mail it back to you. It will not be opened. No one will know what you wrote except you.

But three months from when you finish reading this book you will get a little letter in the mail from you and hopefully that will be a reminder that you are making a valiant effort to turn what some would see as a tragedy into something you see as ultimately a gift -- the gift of insight.

I'm looking forward to receiving your letter and to taking good care of it for a while.

All the best to you and your loved ones.

Namaste!

Suggested Reading

E ACH OF THE books listed below is an outstanding resource for recovering from grief or other major loss.

1. Bridges, William, *Managing Transitions, Making the Most of Change,* Addison Wesley, Reading,1991.
2. Bridges, William, *Transitions, Making Sense of Life's Changes,* Addison Wesley, Reading,1992.
3. Fincher, Susanne F., *Coloring Mandalas for Balance, Harmony, and Spiritual Well-Being,* Shambhala Publications, Inc., Boston, 2004.
4. Gauding, Madonna, *World Mandalas,* Hanchette UK Company, Great Britain, 2005.
5. Grof, Stanislav, M.D., Ph.D., *When the Impossible Happens, Adventures in Non-Ordinary Realities,* Sounds True, Boulder, 2006.
6. James, John W., and Freidman, Russell, *The Grief Recovery Handbook,* Harper Collins, New York, 1998.
7. Hawkins, David R., M.D., Ph.D., *Letting Go: The Pathway of Surrender,* Hay House, Carlsbad, 2012.
8. Hawkins, David R., M.D., Ph.D., *Power vs. Force,* Hay House, Carlsbad, 2002.

9. Longaker, Christine, *Facing Death and Finding Hope,* Main Street, New York, 1997.

10. Tolle, Eckhart, *Stillness Speaks,* New World Library, Novato, 2003.

11. Vaillant, George E., M.D., *Aging Well, Surprising Guideposts to a Happier Life, from the Landmark Harvard Study of Adult Development,* Little, Brown and Company, Boston, 2002.

12. Volkan, Vamik, M.D., and Zintl, Elizabeth, *Life After Loss, the Lessons of Grief,* Charles Scribner's Sons, New York 1993.

13. Weiss, Brian L., M.D., *Many Lives, Many Masters,* Simon & Schuster, New York, 1988.

14. Weiss, Brian L., M.D., and Weiss, Amy E., LCSW, *Miracles Happen, the Transformational Healing Power of Past-Life Memories,* Harper One, New York, 2012.

About the Author

DAYLE E. SPENCER is best known for having been the founding Director of the Conflict Resolution Programs at the Carter Center of Emory University. She worked with former President Jimmy Carter for almost ten years to develop his approaches to negotiating and mediating international conflicts, including civil wars. Carter was awarded the Nobel Peace Prize for these efforts.

Ms. Spencer is a lawyer/negotiator who has organized negotiations between numerous governments and revolutionary leaders in civil war situations, including Ethiopia and Eritrea, Sudan and the Sudanese People's Liberation Front, and Liberia and the National Patriotic Front of Liberia. She is one of the few Americans to have negotiated with the government of North Korea and was instrumental in arranging for peace initiative undertaken by President Carter in that region. Her work in conflict resolution has taken her to over fifty countries on five continents where she has had hands-on involvement in myriad issues.

Prior to her pioneering work at the Carter Center, she served as an Assistant United States Attorney for the Northern District of Alabama and was also law clerk to Chief Judge John R. Brown, of the Fifth US Circuit Court of Appeals in Houston, Texas.

For the past twenty years she has been Managing Director of the Pangaea Group, Inc., where she has served as a consultant to many Fortune 500 companies. Additionally, she and her husband, Will, co-direct the Maui Transitions Center where they assist adults in learning how to manage life's changes.

Dayle has been a frequent commentator on national news broadcasts, published in academic journals as well as authored a nationally syndicated news series on human rights in South Africa, and has tried approximately 100 jury trials in federal district court.

She is the author of *Loving Allie, Transforming the Journey of Loss,* and she blogs on the subject of loss at <u>www.Daylespencer.com</u>. Additionally, she offers *Loving Spirit* workshops for grieving adults.

NOTES

NOTES

NOTES

NOTES

Coming in 2016

Those We Love

Lessons from the
Transformational Journey of Loss

From Dayle Spencer

Loving Allie,
Transforming the Journey of Loss

ISBN: 978-1-4525-2194-7 (sc) $14.99
ISBN: 978-1-4525-2196-1 (hc) $33.99
ISBN: 978-1-4525-2195-4 (e) $3.99

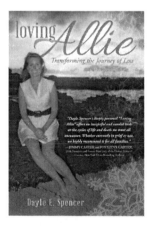

FOR SOME, THE death of a child is a crippling loss. After Mark Twain's daughter, Susan, died at age twenty-four, he famously said, "It is one of the mysteries of our nature that a man, all unprepared, can receive a thunder-stroke like that and live." In *Loving Allie, Transforming the Journey of Loss,* Dayle E. Spencer chronicles how she received such heartbreaking news and how she survived. Part mythological, part autobiographical, part how-to manual, this little book has invaluable insights for anyone who has loved and lost.

CPSIA information can be obtained at www.ICGtesting.com
Printed in the USA
LVOW11s2019160415

434896LV00001B/1/P